PRAISE FOR THE AUTHORS

"The Book of Awesome Latinas is a necessary and joyful correction to the historical record. These stories honor the brilliance and imagination of Latinas who have always shaped our world. More than a celebration of the past, this book fuels hope and power for generations to come." —Katya Echazarreta, Founder of Fundación Espacial and Mexican and American electrical engineer, science communicator, and Citizen Astronaut

The Book of Awesome Latinas is more than just a historical collection; it's a book I wish had existed when I was in college, so I could have known all the work my people have accomplished. This book is a vibrant and essential tribute to the jefas who have shaped the world, often from the shadows. —Author/Illustrator Edward Dennis

"This book is a powerful celebration of Latine brilliance across generations. It is the kind of book every kid, and every adult carrying their inner child, needs on their shelf." — Dr. Esther Zeledon, Author of Creating Your Limitless Life

"Latinas' achievements are VASTLY under celebrated. With this book, we're reminded of how remarkable Latinas are and have been, and we're reclaiming our mark in history across every industry. It's a must-read!" — Liz Rebecca Alarcón, Founder & CEO @ProjectPulso

"As timely as it is urgent, The Book of Awesome Latinas arrives at a moment when our community needs, more than ever, to take control of the narrative. These stories remind us that our legacy has always been built in real time, through resilience, imagination, and sheer will. For every woman of color looking for inspiration or a reason to keep showing up, this book belongs on your shelf." — Yamily Habib, Editorial Director, mitu

"More than ever, we all need to be reminded of the Latinas who not only dreamt of a better world, but committed their lives to ensure it became a reality. This book will inspire Latinas everywhere to believe that they, too, can be the change!" — Cat Lantigua, Author of Build It and They Will Come: A Guide to Architecting Intentional Community

"These stories of Latina innovators are not footnotes to history; they are history. Whether through bold confrontation or quiet disruption, the women in these pages did what women have always done when systems fail them: they built something better.

This book doesn't just celebrate Latina excellence - it corrects the record and invites all of us women into the work of shattering ceilings of every kind. I have found this book essential and deeply inspiring." — Keren Eldad, author of Gilded: Breaking Free from the Cage of Ambition, Perfectionism, and the Relentless Pursuit of More

"This dazzling anthology of Latina trailblazers, The Book Of Awesome Latinas, by Ashley K. Stoyanov Ojeda and Mirtle Peña-Calderón, is written with passion and purpose, with the hope that readers will catch their Latina fire: to hope, to dream, and achieve. Spanning centuries and countries of Latin and North American, it contains scores of Latinas' powerful stories in mini-biographies across all fields of human endeavor, of amazing feminists who rose against the odds to share their light with their sisterhood. Join the circle of las mujeres indomables and be inspired as you read and share this vital book, one missing too long from our shelves." — Kate Farrell, story-teller, author, Story Power and The Fairy Tale Heroine: Live and Write Her Journey

"Reading 'The Book of Awesome Latinas' feels like being reminded of who we are and why our stories matter. These profiles honor the women who paved the way, often without credit, and affirm that Latina brilliance has always existed. This book restores our place in history while inspiring pride and possibility for the next generation."

—Delsy Sandoval, Co-Host and Co-Executive Producer of Tamarindo Podcast, and Executive Producer of Ocu-Pasión Podcast

"For too long, Latinas have been made to believe we don't have a history or heroines to be proud of, just the same few names and faces endlessly recycled by media that was never interested in telling the whole story. The Book of Awesome Latinas breaks that pattern. Spanning Latin America, the Caribbean, and the Latina diaspora, this book celebrates the oft-forgotten change-makers, artists, innovators, barrier-breakers, and freedom fighters who shaped our past and are redefining our future. These are the stories that were overlooked, minimized, or never taught at all — until now." —Raquel Reichard, author of "Self-Care for Latinas" and Deputy Director at Somos by Refinery29

THE BOOK OF AWESOME LATINAS

FROM PASSIONATE PIONEERS TO UNSTOPPABLE INNOVATORS

ASHLEY K. STOYANOV OJEDA

MIRTLE PEÑA-CALDERÓN

Published by Books That Save Lives, an imprint of Jim Dandy Publishing, LLC

Cover Design: Carmen Fortunato
Illustrations: Maclin Lisle

Published by BTSL/Jim Dandy Publishing
6252 Peach Avenue
Van Nuys, CA 91411
info@jimdandypublishing.com

For bulk orders, special quantities, course adoptions, and corporate sales, please email info@jimdandypublishing.com

ISBN: (print) 9781684817955, (ebook) 9781684817962

BISAC: SOC044000, BIO022000, HIS068000

CONTENTS

To all the women in our families,
our amigas,
the women we have yet to meet,
those yet to be born,
those we have lost,
and to all the jefas who have
ever doubted the strength of their voices
and kept on just the same.

WORD FROM THE AUTHORS

De Ashley:

I'll be honest: Before writing this book, I was never much of a history buff. But co-authoring this project has completely shifted how I see history and my place in it. Along this journey, one truth has only become clearer: Our stories matter, and we need to tell them. That's all history really is:stories. And the unfortunate reality is that so many of the powerful, courageous, selfless Latinas you'll meet in these pages have been forgotten, erased, or deliberately written out because their countries were too intimidated by the impact they made.

These women weren't just participants in history:they were leaders who made real *jefa* moves that others were too scared to make. They sacrificed everything:their reputations, their families, even their lives:for justice. They stood in the fire, demanded change, and carved out possibilities for generations who came after them.

I've always been proud to be Latina. I've always known our ancestors paved the way for us. But writing this book has made me realize just how strong they were, and how much we owe to their determination. I am profoundly grateful to these women:for their lives, their courage, and the chance to showcase their stories here.

My hope is that their stories don't just live on in these pages, but continue to inspire you to learn more, to dive deeper into the histories of your own countries, and to uncover the names and voices that were left behind. This book is here to teach, but I also hope it pushes you toward action:to take change into your own hands, just as these Latinas did.

Because, at the end of the day, we are just as capable of being power-ful, brave, and brilliant as they were. And we owe it to them:and to ourselves:to be nothing less.

So here's to these AWESOME LATINAS. *Y adelante!*

De Mirtle:

I love our culture. It's vibrant, resilient, and incredibly human. As someone who has enjoyed learning history all of her life:whether it was because I was being a *chismosa* or just loved wrapping myself up into a narrative:there was always the gnawing feeling of wondering where all the women were. You see all the great achieve-ments of the men, but not enough of the women. It's not to say that men can't do great things; they most definitely can, but so can women.

Over the last few years, I've learned that women, regardless of their creed, background, or lived experience, are stronger together. Women:and, for this book, Latinas:are monumentally exquisite beings. They are capable of anything and everything, save a few things. When Ashley and I teamed up for this project, there was a silent understanding that this book would serve as a small compila-tion of all the things Latinas have done and are capable of doing. That this book would remind all Latinas that they are magnificent and enough. How they can be inspired to do the hard things because it is deeply ingrained in their DNA.

Latinas are glorious in their power, resilient and strong. They leave me in awe, wondering how I can draw energy from them to pursue my dreams and aspirations. They remind me that all we ever truly need is a small spark for the magic to make its way to us.

This book has made me think about my *abuelas*, Olga, Margarita, and Petra. Olga was a woman filled with dreams and aspirations who dedicated her life to raising four boys, one of whom I am blessed to call my *papi*. Margarita was a woman who devoted her life to education, becoming the principal of a school, and along the way, had four children of her own, one of whom became my *mami*. And then, there's the spitfire who is Petra, a woman who left her home country because she knew her girls would have a better life elsewhere.

Both Olga and Margarita passed long ago, and Petra's memories have faded. I have wondered tirelessly what they would think about this book. Would they be proud? Would they show everyone a copy of it? Given how my parents and *tías* turned out, I'd like to think they would.

I also wonder what their lives would have been if they'd had the support and resources that Latinas have today. What would Olga's two daughters, whom she never got to see grow into women, have been like? What would they have achieved? How would Margarita have guided her two daughters and several granddaughters if she had had more time? How would she have celebrated them and their achievements? How much further could Petra have gotten with her brilliant mind if it weren't for societal constraints?

This got me thinking about my *tías*, *primas*, *amigas*, and every single Latina out there. What could we all do if we knew more about what we were capable of? How could we change the world? I think about my nieces and the women they will one day become.

I write this book for the Latinas yet to be born:the ones still stardust waiting to come down to earth. I do it for the ones whose families crossed borders to ensure they had a better life. For those whose families assimilated as a form of survival and who never had the opportunity to learn Spanish. I do this for them. Every single one of them.

Each of them inspires me and gives me hope. Each of them fills me with passion and love. Each of them reminds me of my *poder*. Researching the women we wanted to include in this book was a daunting task because there are so many more we want to mention, and simply can't.

My hope with this book is that we open the scope of Latinahood so much wider than it has ever been.

We want to show that we've been killing it since the dawn of time. We want to show that Latinas have been showing up and taking names:to show how, regardless of our circumstances, we have been a steady heartbeat within our culture, our families, and our lives. Latinas are made of the tough stuff. They are made of the right stuff:the stuff that is powered by this unquenchable and unquestionable force.

But, for too long, we have been left out of the narrative. Our stories are left by the wayside and ignored because someone has deemed them not important enough. We all know that's a bold-faced deception that has begun to crack over time. Latinas are here, and we deserve and demand to be heard.

We are a flame that no one can put out, and for all of you, I will gladly carry the torch you lit the moment you set foot on this earth. Your light, song, and melody will be heard loud and clear, without interruption. There is a magical hum in the air that is as stunning and brilliant as *la rosa de Bayahíbe* and the *dalia*. You will take flight just like *la cigua palmera* and the *águila real*.

I want to thank every single woman in this book, the ones not in this book, my *tías*, my *primas*, my *amigas*, my *abuelas*, my co-author, and, most importantly, my parents. Without you, there is no me, there is no book.

INTRODUCTION

For much of history, the achievements of women have been categorically pushed aside in favor of the celebration of men. While men have done things that are worthy of praise, so have women. Things like the Kevlar vest, CCTV, the precursor to Wi-Fi technology, and the first computer algorithm were all created by industrious women who identified a societal pain point and sought to fix it.

This is no different for scores of trailblazing and innovative Latinas who have fought injustice, misogyny, and systemic oppression. Latinas have always been seen as fierce, fiery, outspoken, and determined. It's a stereotype that has followed them for centuries, and one that is both true and untrue. Where some Latinas fight fire with fire, others have been known to take more subtle approaches:each ending with the same result: change.

None of the women in this book started with the idea that they would make history on the scale they did; their ultimate goal was to create a more equitable society where Latinas (and women in general) could achieve their fullest potential without the hindrance of a glass ceiling.

.

Latinas walk hand in hand with the strength, history, and dreams of their ancestors as well as the future of those who will follow them. When one of us wins, when one of us achieves monumental feats of success, we all do.

"We have to tell our stories. We have to be visible. We have to be counted."

—*Maria Hinojosa, a Mexican-American journalist and executive producer of Latino USA, as well as the founder of Futuro Media Group, and winner of a Pulitzer Prize*

ONE
KEEPERS OF JUSTICE
ACTIVISTS AND ADVOCATES

Throughout history, women's rights have been systematically denied, erased, or never acknowledged to begin with. The systems in place were never built for equality, and while progress has been made, the fight is far from over. The women in this chapter refused to accept the status quo. They were not content with silence, oppression, or injustice. Instead, they fought:often at great personal cost:to challenge oppressive governments, outdated traditions, and deep-seated discrimination. Some were exiled, others survived assassination attempts, and many risked everything to demand a better future for the generations that followed.

These women did not just fight for justice:they paved the way for us, present-day Latinas, who also want to create change in our own corners of the world. Their struggles remind us that progress is never given; it is demanded, fought for, and sometimes even died for. As you read their stories, ask yourself: Who do I resonate with? Why? Maybe this is the beginning of your own activism and advocacy journey. Let their courage inspire you, fuel you, and motivate you to take action:because the fight for justice is far from over.

ESTELA DE CARLOTTO

LA ABUELA QUE NUNCA SE RINDIÓ

In the face of unimaginable loss, Estela de Carlotto turned her grief into an unstoppable movement for truth, justice, and memory. As the president of *Abuelas de Plaza de Mayo*, she has dedicated her life to searching for the children stolen during Argentina's brutal dictatorship (1976–1983). Her story is one of resilience, courage, and the power of a determined Latina who refused to stay silent.

Estela wasn't always a human rights activist. Born in 1930 in Buenos Aires, she was a schoolteacher and a mother who lived a quiet life:until history tore her family apart. In 1977, her twenty-three-year-old daughter, Laura Estela Carlotto, was kidnapped by the military regime while pregnant. Laura was held in captivity and gave birth to a baby boy before being murdered by the government. Her child, like an estimated five hundred others, was taken and illegally adopted by families connected to the dictatorship.

In that year, Estela and a group of courageous women came together to form *Abuelas de Plaza de Mayo*. Their mission was clear: find their missing grandchildren, restore their true identities, and demand justice. These *abuelas*:who once might have been expected to stay in the background:became fierce advocates, standing in the public eye, marching every Thursday in the Plaza de Mayo, and fearlessly challenging those in power.

For decades, Estela searched for her grandson. She became a symbol of perseverance, taking her fight beyond Argentina's borders, advocating for DNA testing, and ensuring that history would never forget the atrocities committed during the dictatorship. Then, in 2014:after thirty-six years of searching:she received the call she had been waiting for. Her grandson, Guido Montoya Carlotto, had discovered his true identity.

Her victory was personal, but her fight continues. *Abuelas de Plaza de Mayo* has helped recover the identities of over 130 stolen grandchildren, yet many more remain missing. Today, Estela, in her nineties, is still a force to be reckoned with. She reminds us that memory is resistance, and that no matter how much time passes, *la verdad siempre sale a la luz*:the truth always comes out.

Her legacy is one of love and defiance:a testament to the strength of a *jefa* who refused to let injustice win.

LAURA INÉS POLLÁN TOLEDO

The Woman Who Dared to Wear White

In a country where dissent was met with silence:or violence:Laura Inés Pollán Toledo refused to be quiet. A schoolteacher by trade, she became a symbol of resistance when the Cuban government jailed her husband, independent journalist Héctor Maseda, during the Black Spring of 2003. Instead of retreating into fear, she took to the streets. She founded *Las Damas de Blanco* (The Ladies in White), a movement of wives, mothers, and daughters of political prisoners who peacefully demanded their loved ones' freedom.

Every Sunday, dressed in white and carrying gladiolus flowers:symbols of strength and perseverance:Laura and the other women marched through Havana, enduring harassment from government-organized mobs. They were shouted at, pushed, even arrested, but they never backed down. "The authorities have three options," Laura once declared. "Free our husbands, imprison us, or kill us."

The Cuban government tried to erase her. They labeled her a "traitor" and launched smear campaigns in the state media. But despite years of intimidation, beatings, and arrests, she remained committed to nonviolent resistance. In 2005, *Las Damas de Blanco* won the Sakharov Prize for Freedom of Thought, one of the highest honors in the world for human rights activism. But the Cuban government barred her from leaving the island to accept it.

By 2010, after years of unrelenting protests, many of the imprisoned dissidents:including her husband:were released. But Laura wasn't done. She knew the problem was bigger than just those seventy-five men; Cuba's laws hadn't changed, and new political prisoners were being thrown behind bars. She kept marching, kept organizing, kept resisting.

Then, suddenly, she was gone. On October 7, 2011, Laura was hospitalized with a respiratory illness. Just a week later, she was dead. Official reports claimed she died of cardiac arrest. Still, many believe her death was no accident, described as "death by purposeful medical neglect" in the custody of Cuban State Security at the Hospital Calixto García in Havana. The Cuban government had found a way to silence her permanently.

Her loss was a devastating blow, but her movement did not die with her. *Las Damas de Blanco* continued their weekly marches, renaming themselves *Las Damas de Blanco Laura Pollán* in her honor. Today, more than three hundred women across Cuba carry forward her fight for justice, proving that Laura's voice:like her courage:can never truly be silenced. She showed the world that, even in the face of dictatorship, dignity and resistance could still shine through:as bright as a white dress against the darkness of oppression.

BERTA CÁCERES

THE WARRIOR WHO DEFENDED THE RIVERS

Some leaders are born from history, others from necessity. Berta Cáceres was both. A proud Lenca woman from Honduras, she dedicated her life to defending Indigenous land, rivers, and rights:and paid the ultimate price for it.

Berta was raised in La Esperanza, Honduras, by her mother, Austra Bertha Flores, a midwife, activist, and politician who sheltered refugees from El Salvador. From an early age, Berta witnessed both injustice and resistance, shaping her into the fearless leader she became. In 1993, when she was just nineteen, she co-founded COPINH (*Consejo Cívico de Organizaciones Populares e Indígenas de Honduras*) to fight for Indigenous rights, environmental justice, and territorial sovereignty.

In 2006, Lenca community members from Río Blanco approached COPINH with alarming news: Heavy machinery and construction workers had arrived without warning. They soon learned that the Agua Zarca Dam project, backed by powerful corporations and the Honduran government, was set to divert the sacred Gualcarque River:a lifeline for their people.

Berta launched a grassroots resistance movement, filing legal complaints, mobilizing international organizations, and organizing a human blockade to stop the dam's construction. The blockade lasted over a year, despite violent repression. Protesters were threatened, beaten, even killed: including Tomás García, a fellow Indigenous leader, shot by the military during a peaceful protest.

But Berta never backed down. Her fight forced Sinohydro, the world's largest dam developer, and the International Finance Corporation (the private arm of the World Bank) to withdraw from the project. She had done the impossible: She stopped a megaproject with the power of the people.

Her victories came at a cost. Threats against her life intensified. She was arrested multiple times, branded a traitor, and constantly watched. Still, she continued organizing, warning the world about Honduras's growing attacks on environmental defenders.

Then, on March 3, 2016, armed men broke into her home and assassinated her in her sleep. Twelve days later, her colleague Nelson García was also murdered. International outrage erupted. In 2018, a Honduran court ruled that executives from DESA, the company behind the dam, had ordered her killing. Seven men were convicted, but the masterminds behind her murder remain in power.

Though she was silenced, her fight continues. COPINH remains active, and Berta's family still demands full justice. Around the world, environmental activists invoke her name as a symbol of resistance, courage, and Indigenous power.

Berta Cáceres taught us that the fight for land and water is a fight for life itself. And, like a river, her legacy cannot be stopped.

LUCÍA IXCHÍU

DEFENDING THE LAND WITH ART AND RESISTANCE

For Lucía Ixchíu, activism isn't just about fighting:it's about creating. A K'iche' Maya journalist, artist, and feminist, she has used art, music, and storytelling to challenge oppression, defend Indigenous rights, and honor Guatemala's historical memory. She believes that resistance is not just about protest, but also about building a new world, one that respects Indigenous sovereignty, the environment, and human dignity.

Lucía's journey began at thirteen, when she and her sister organized rock concerts in their hometown. But her activism took a deeper turn on October 4, 2012, when the Guatemalan military massacred seven Indigenous protesters on the Summit of Alaska. The victims had been peacefully demonstrating against rising electricity rates and constitutional changes that threatened Indigenous communities.

The government and mainstream media twisted the narrative, blaming the victims instead of the perpetrators. Furious at the injustice, Lucía decided to tell the truth herself. Two weeks after the massacre, she became a journalist:not because she had formal training, but because she had a story to tell.

Her student group at San Carlos University staged a protest, covering the government palace in red paint to symbolize the bloodshed. The response? Persecution. Five students, including Lucía, were targeted by the government of Otto Pérez Molina, accused of crimes for speaking out.

At first, writing terrified her. Like many Indigenous people, she had been conditioned to believe her voice didn't matter. "Since colonial times, Indigenous people have been treated like animals," she said. "I inherited this low self-esteem." But her anger became her power. The rage of five hundred years of oppression fueled her words, and soon she saw that journalism was a tool of resistance.

But journalism alone wasn't enough. In 2013, when her fellow activists were jailed for their political work, she and others asked: What can we do to help? The answer? Music.

One of her friends had a rock band, and Lucía was a cultural promoter. Together, they organized a solidarity concert to raise funds for political prisoners. That event became a movement: *Festivales Solidarios* (Solidarity Festivals), a collective that uses art, culture, and public events to defend Indigenous rights and challenge criminalization.

For Lucía, art and activism are inseparable. Through *Festivales Solidarios*, she has organized poetry readings, film screenings, and artistic caravans that travel to various communities, bringing creative resistance to the front lines of struggle.

But this work comes at a price. Lucía has been beaten, detained, defamed, and even survived an assassination attempt. Her activism forced her into exile, but even outside of Guatemala, she continues to organize. She co-founded *La Colmena*, a traveling school that teaches art, journalism, and communication to young activists. She also coordinates the Movement for Black and Indigenous Liberation, working with grassroots organizations across the Americas.

Despite criminalization and exile, Lucía refuses to stop. She dreams of returning home, of a Guatemala where art and activism thrive, and where defending the land is no longer a crime. Until then, she continues to fight:from the streets, from digital platforms, and through the stories she tells.

Her message is clear: Art is not just for expression:it is for revolution.

BERTHA OLIVA NATIVÍ: FIGHTING FOR THE TRUTH AND JUSTICE

For Bertha Oliva Nativi, the fight for human rights is personal. In 1981, her husband, Tomás Nativí, was disappeared by Honduras's military death squads, leaving her pregnant and alone. Instead of succumbing to fear, she turned her pain into action, becoming one of the most prominent human rights defenders in Central America. She co-founded COFADEH (*Comité de Familiares de Detenidos Desaparecidos en Honduras*), an organization that has spent over forty years seeking justice for victims of disappearance and state violence.

On June 11, 1981, hooded men:agents of the military dictatorship:stormed her home. Her husband, a revolutionary activist, was taken. She never saw him again. Left behind, blindfolded and bound, she made a decision: She would fight to uncover the truth and demand justice.

She soon realized she was not alone. Other families were also searching for husbands, sons, daughters, and siblings who had vanished. Together, they founded COFADEH, determined to hold the government accountable for the more than five hundred disappearances between 1979 and 1989.

Though Honduras's military dictatorship officially ended, state repression never stopped. Bertha has spent decades exposing extrajudicial killings, illegal detentions, and the criminalization of activism. Her fight intensified after the 2009 coup that ousted President Manuel Zelaya, when human rights violations surged once again. She became a leading voice in the resistance movement, denouncing abuses committed by security forces against journalists, Indigenous leaders, and political dissidents.

Her work has made her a target. She has endured threats, surveillance, and smear campaigns, yet she refuses to back down. "I had two options: to live in fear or to continue the struggle. I chose the struggle."

Bertha understands that impunity fuels continued violence. That's why COFADEH not only documents human rights abuses, but also preserves the stories of the disappeared, ensuring that their names and their struggles are never forgotten.

Nearly four decades after her husband's disappearance, she still searches for the truth and hopes to find his remains. But her mission is larger than her personal loss:she fights for all victims of state violence, past and present.

Today, Bertha remains one of the most powerful voices for human rights in Honduras. She has built coalitions, trained new generations of activists, and taken the fight for justice to international courts. As long as impunity reigns, she will continue her work:for the disappeared, for the persecuted, and for those who can no longer speak for themselves.

EUFROSINA CRUZ

DEFYING TRADITION TO PAVE A PATH FOR OTHERS

In 2007, Eufrosina Cruz made history by winning the mayoral election in her hometown of Santa María Quiegolani, Oaxaca. But instead of swearing her in, male electoral officials annulled her victory, claiming that as a woman, she had no right to lead. They even destroyed the ballots that showed she had won. This blatant injustice didn't silence her:it ignited her fight to break down the barriers keeping Indigenous women from power.

Eufrosina's journey to political activism started long before that stolen election. She was born into a Zapotec Indigenous community where women were expected to stay in the home, and be married off as teenagers, denied education, and excluded from decision-making. At just seven years old, she realized the deep inequality when her teacher let her play marbles with the boys, an act forbidden to girls.

When she was twelve, her father made the difficult decision to let her leave their village to study, a rare and courageous choice in a community where most girls never got the chance. It was outside of her hometown that she learned Spanish, discovered her rights, and understood that she could demand a different future.

After her mayoral victory was stolen, Eufrosina refused to accept that Indigenous women could be erased from politics. She founded the Association for Gender Unity, Integrity, and Equality of Oaxaca (Quiego). She successfully fought to change Article 25 in 2010, securing women's right to vote and run for office in her state. This reform was adopted by the United Nations in 2014. She went on to become the first Indigenous woman elected to the Oaxacan legislature, and later served as a Federal Deputy in the Mexican Congress.

Beyond voting rights, Eufrosina also helped pass a law criminalizing child marriage, tackling a practice in which girls were often traded for dowries of beer, animals, or money. Today, 70% of her hometown's municipal council is made up of women:a sign of how much has changed.

While she proudly embraces her Indigenous identity, she argues that tradition should never be used to justify oppression. "Mexico has to learn to look at Indigenous people with new eyes," she says. "We are not vulnerable:we are powerful."

Eufrosina has taken her fight beyond politics, sharing her story on global platforms. In her TEDx talk, "How I Claimed the Rights Life Had Denied Me," she speaks about overcoming discrimination through education and breaking cultural paradigms.

She also captured her journey in her bestselling book, *Los sueños de la niña de la montaña* (*The Dreams of the Mountain Girl*). Writing it was painful:reliving hunger, exclusion, and injustice:but it also allowed her to forgive her father, her circumstances, and even herself. She hopes the book will inspire young Indigenous girls to take control of their future.

Eufrosina Cruz has transformed the landscape for Indigenous women in Mexico, proving that bravery and determination can rewrite history.

RIGOBERTA MENCHÚ TUM

THE *GUERRERA* WHO USED HER STORY AS ACTIVISM

Rigoberta Menchú is a Guatemalan Indigenous activist whose fight for justice has made her one of the most influential human rights defenders in the world. Born in 1959 into the Quiché Maya community, she grew up witnessing extreme poverty, forced labor, and violent repression against Indigenous people. By the time she was a teenager, she had already lost two brothers to malnutrition and illness. During Guatemala's brutal civil war, the military assassinated her father, mother, and another brother. These atrocities fueled her determination to resist.

Menchú began her activism by joining the Peasant Unity Committee (CUC), an organization fighting for Indigenous land rights and labor protections. She became a key organizer, uniting Guatemala's twenty-two Indigenous groups in their struggle against violent oppression. However, her activism put her life in danger, and in 1981, she was forced into exile in Mexico. There, she continued to advocate for her people on the international stage.

One of her most impactful contributions was the publication of her autobiography, *I, Rigoberta Menchú: An Indian Woman in Guatemala* (1983). The book exposed the horrors of Guatemala's civil war and the genocide against Indigenous people. It became a global sensation, drawing widespread attention to the human rights crisis in Guatemala and pressuring the international community to act.

In 1992, Menchú was awarded the Nobel Peace Prize, becoming the first Indigenous woman to receive the honor. She used the prize money to establish the Rigoberta Menchú Tum Foundation, which promotes Indigenous rights, cultural preservation, and justice for victims of human rights abuses. One of her most significant achievements was pushing for legal action against former Guatemalan military leaders.

In 1999, she filed charges in Spain against ex-dictators for crimes of genocide, torture, and terrorism:marking one of the first major efforts to hold Latin American war criminals accountable in international courts. This legal battle laid the groundwork for the historic conviction of former dictator Efraín Ríos Montt of the crime of genocide in 2013:the first time a former head of state was found guilty of such crimes in their own country.

Though the ruling was overturned, it set a precedent for Indigenous-led justice movements worldwide. Menchú continues her work today through her foundation and as a co-founder of the Nobel Women's Initiative, advocating for Indigenous communities and women's rights globally.

Despite controversy surrounding her autobiography and political career, her legacy as a *guerrera*:one who defied both personal tragedy and systemic oppression:remains undeniable.

KARLA AVELAR

THE SURVIVOR WHO DID NOT GIVE UP THE FIGHT FOR TRANS RIGHTS

Karla Avelar is a Salvadoran transgender activist who has defied the odds to become a powerful advocate for human rights. Born into a deeply conservative and impoverished Catholic family in 1978, she endured relentless violence from an early age. By the time she was ten, she had already survived sexual abuse and been forced to flee her home, and was living on the streets of San Salvador.

As a trans woman in El Salvador:a country where gang violence, government repression, and extreme discrimination make survival nearly impossible:Avelar has faced near-constant threats to her life. She has survived two shootings, a stabbing, prolonged periods of incarceration marked by abuse and servitude, and years without access to HIV treatment. Despite this, she has transformed her suffering into action, becoming a fearless advocate for the rights of trans people, prisoners, and individuals living with HIV.

In 1992, Avelar was shot nine times by one of the serial killers known as the *Matalocas*, a high-ranking military officer who had been targeting trans women in San Salvador. She miraculously survived after weeks in a coma, only to wake up to the devastating news that she was HIV-positive.

This was the first attempt on her life, but it would not be the last. In 2006, gang members shot her five times for refusing to pay extortion fees while doing sex work. When she survived, they tried to finish the job the following year, stabbing her twice in the back while she was speaking to a client. Even after enduring so much violence, Avelar refused to back down. She decided to fight not just for her own survival, but for the safety and dignity of the entire trans community.

In 2008, Avelar founded COMCAVIS Trans (*Comunidad Comunicando y Capacitando a Mujeres Trans con VIH en El Salvador*), the first organization in El Salvador dedicated to supporting trans women living with HIV. Through COMCAVIS, she has worked tirelessly to secure better healthcare, legal protections, and visibility for trans people, particularly those in prison or facing extreme marginalization.

One of her most impactful victories was advocating for reforms at Sensuntepeque prison, where she had been incarcerated between 1996 and 2000. During her imprisonment, trans women were subjected to daily sexual violence, forced labor, and abuse from both inmates and guards. After her release, Avelar filed formal complaints that led to the establishment of Sector 2, a separate unit within the prison providing a safer space for trans and gay inmates.

Her activism helped secure fundamental rights for incarcerated trans women, including access to hormone therapy, the right to wear gender-affirming clothing, and protections from gang violence inside the prison system.

In 2013, she became the first trans woman to testify before the Inter-American Commission on Human Rights (IACHR), exposing the state-sanctioned violence against LGBTQ+ individuals in El Salvador. She later took her advocacy to the United Nations, where she played a key role in securing the first-ever UN recommendations addressing LGBTI discrimination in El Salvador. In 2017, she was nominated for the Martin Ennals Award for Human Rights Defenders, an international recognition of her fearless work.

Despite ongoing death threats and political persecution, Avelar refuses to leave El Salvador, believing that her fight is far from over. She continues to demand justice for the countless trans people who have been murdered, disappeared, or forced into exile. For her, activism is not just a choice:it is a necessity.

DOLORES HUERTA

THE WOMAN WHO ORGANIZED A MOVEMENT

Dolores Huerta is one of the most influential labor activists in US history. This civil rights leader transformed the lives of farmworkers through relentless organizing, legislative victories, and her unwavering belief in collective power. As the co-founder of the United Farm Workers (UFW) alongside César Chávez, Huerta shaped the modern labor rights movement, proving that grassroots activism could challenge deeply entrenched systems of exploitation. Her legacy is one of courage, resilience, and a lifelong commitment to justice.

Born in 1930 in Dawson, New Mexico, Huerta's early life was shaped by her mother's compassion and strong work ethic. Raised in Stockton, California, she saw firsthand the struggles of agricultural workers and the racism faced by Latinos. A teacher by training, she left the profession when she realized she could do more to help farmworker families through activism than in the classroom.

"I couldn't tolerate seeing kids come to class hungry and needing shoes," she later recalled.

Determined to create change, she joined the Community Service Organization (CSO), where she met César Chávez. Their shared vision for farmworker rights led them to break away from the CSO in 1962 to form the National Farm Workers Association (NFWA), which later became the UFW.

Huerta's activism was bold and strategic. In 1965, she was instrumental in organizing the Delano grape strike, which brought together Filipino and Mexican farmworkers in a historic five-year struggle for fair wages and conditions. She led the national grape boycott that followed, rallying millions of Americans to stand in solidarity with farmworkers.

At its peak, an estimated seventeen million people stopped buying grapes, leading to the first successful union contracts for farm laborers. Throughout her career, Huerta was also a key advocate for safer working conditions, pushing for the elimination of harmful pesticides and securing unemployment and healthcare benefits for farmworkers.

Despite her immense contributions, Huerta's work was often overshadowed by Chávez, and she faced sexism both within the movement and from the opposition. She endured brutal attacks:most notably in 1988, when she was beaten by San Francisco police officers at a peaceful protest, breaking several ribs and rupturing her spleen. Yet she never wavered. She coined the iconic slogan *Sí se puede* (Yes we can), a phrase that became a rallying cry not only for farmworkers, but for movements around the world.

Huerta's impact extends beyond labor rights. She has been a fierce advocate for women's rights, Latinx representation in politics, and civic engagement. In 2003, she founded the Dolores Huerta Foundation, continuing to empower communities through grassroots organizing and leadership development. Her dedication has earned her numerous honors, including the Eleanor Roosevelt Human Rights Award and the Presidential Medal of Freedom.

Now in her nineties, Huerta remains a force for change. Her life's work is a testament to the power of organizing, the importance of intersectional activism, and the belief that when people come together, they can create a more just world. *Sí se puede*:and thanks to Dolores Huerta, we know it to be true.

SERAFINA DÁVALOS

THE CHANGEMAKING LAWYER THEY TRIED TO ERASE

Born in 1883 in Ajos (now Coronel Oviedo), Serafina Dávalos was the first woman to graduate from the Faculty of Law at the Universidad Nacional de Asunción in 1907. But her ambition extended far beyond earning a degree:Dávalos was a trailblazer for gender equality, legal rights, and feminist thought in Latin America.

At a time when Paraguayan women were denied the right to vote, and when marriage was widely seen as their sole destiny, Dávalos challenged the very foundations of patriarchy, arguing for women's legal, political, and social equality.

Her path was never easy. When she finished secondary school, there were no opportunities for women to pursue higher education in Paraguay. Instead of accepting this reality, Dávalos, along with other graduates, petitioned the government to create a teacher training school for women. This effort was successful, enabling her to earn a teaching diploma in 1898. This early activism foreshadowed the rest of her life: Where she saw injustice, she acted.

Dávalos' landmark 1907 thesis, *Humanismo*, was a groundbreaking critique of Paraguay's legal and cultural systems through a feminist lens. She argued that a true democracy could not exist without gender equality, and demanded an end to the idea that women's primary role was one of submission in the home.

Her assertion that marriage was a form of enslavement for women was radical for its time, and sparked intense backlash from Paraguay's big players. Yet her work laid the foundation for feminist movements in the country. Decades later, in recognition of its importance, *Humanismo* was republished after being lost for eighty-four years.

Beyond academia, Dávalos was an active organizer and leader. She co-founded the *Centro Feminista Paraguayo* and played a key role in the *Unión Femenina del Paraguay* and the *Liga Paraguaya Pro Derechos de la Mujer*. She represented Paraguay at the *Primer Congreso Femenino Internacional* in Buenos Aires in 1910, where she was elected to the *Federación Panamericana de Mujeres*, further amplifying her advocacy for women's rights on an international scale.

Her influence extended into the legal realm as well, where she was appointed to the *Superior Tribunal de Justicia* (a high-ranking court in the Paraguayan government), a rare achievement for a woman at the time.

She was known for walking proudly through Asunción, defying conventions not only as an outspoken feminist, but also as a woman who openly lived with her partner, Honoria Barilán. In a deeply conservative Catholic society, her refusal to conform and be a part of the LGBTQ+ community led to her erasure from historical narratives. When she passed away in 1957, she was denied a religious burial, and her resting place was left unmarked:an attempt to obscure her legacy.

But history has refused to forget Serafina Dávalos. Today, feminist scholars, activists, and historians work to recover and honor her contributions. She was not just Paraguay's first female lawyer:she was a revolutionary thinker, a feminist pioneer, and a woman who demanded that her country see women as full citizens. Over a century later, her fight for equality continues to inspire.

"They are afraid of us because we are not afraid of them."

BERTA CÁCERES, A HONDURAN
ENVIRONMENTAL ACTIVIST, INDIGENOUS
LEADER, CO-FOUNDER AND COORDINATOR
OF THE COUNCIL OF POPULAR AND
INDIGENOUS ORGANIZATIONS OF HONDURAS

TWO
LITERARY LIGHTS
WRITERS, POETS, AND STORYTELLERS

Stories have the power to transport us to places we've never been before and evoke emotions outside of what we are used to. When a story is in the right hands, the power it holds can rewrite our DNA in a way that leaves us in a distinctly different state of being. For much of human history, storytelling has been a means to foster connections between the past and the present. It was a way to teach people what mistakes to avoid, while simultaneously reminding them of what is truly possible when you believe.

One phrase, one sentence, one paragraph, or one page can lead you down a path you wouldn't suspect. You can meet people who look and think differently from you. There is a magic stored within those pages, all waiting to be unlocked right before your eyes. They want to hold you close, show you the truest meaning of life, and then release you so that you may hold yourself up differently.

That powerful feeling can only come at the hands of someone who is skilled and holds the multitude of human emotions within their soul. The women in this chapter don't just hold entire worlds within their heads; they carry entire universes, all waiting to be explored. All waiting to be shared. All waiting to be loved.

GABRIELA MISTRAL: LA DAMA DE LA DESOLACIÓN, EL AMOR Y LA COMPASIÓN

To live is to experience a multitude of emotions and events that can leave lasting scars. Where some take that and internalize it, others take it and create everlasting magic that transcends time and generations. Gabriela was a poet, author, and educator who took the hardships that life placed before her and used them to learn to fly.

Born in Vicuña, Chile, on April 7, 1889, as Lucila de María del Perpetuo Socorro Godoy Alcayaga, she grew up with her mother and older sister. Though not a steadfast figure in her life, her father, a poetry-writing schoolteacher, was said to have inspired a great sense of creativity and passion for literature. At a young age, she was sent away to school, where she was mistreated by teachers who felt she was a troublemaker. Gabriela was said to have started writing poetry after the passing of her great love.

By 1914, she had published *Sonetos de la Muerte*, which were love poems she wrote to honor those who had passed on. These garnered her much renown, but it wasn't until she published her collections of poems in *Desolación* (1922) that her renown spread even further. She published the childhood-themed collection *Ternura* in 1924, followed by *Tala* sometime later.

While writing and publishing some of her most significant collections, Gabriela continued to work within the school system, eventually rising through the ranks and overseeing schools. During this time, she witnessed injustice and mistreatment of local communities. This, along with the mistreatment she experienced as a child, heavily influenced her writing, as she was a champion for children and those who could not fend for themselves.

After publishing *Desolación*, she began traveling more and giving lectures, which led her to relocate to Mexico sometime after the Mexican Revolution to help rebuild the school system there. By the time she published her second book, she had already left Mexico and become active in international politics. This eventually led her to become the Chilean consul in Naples, Madrid, and Lisbon.

In 1945, she became the first Latin American to receive the Nobel Prize for Literature. She also held honorary degrees from the University of Florence and the University of Guatemala. Gabriela also taught Spanish literature in the United States at Columbia University, Middlebury College, Vassar College, and the University of Puerto Rico.

After having lived a life filled with deep emotion and great reward, she passed away in New York on January 10, 1957, due to complications of pancreatic cancer.

ISABEL ALLENDE: THE DAUGHTER OF FORTUNE, SOUL, AND PROSE

It is said that the pen is mightier than the sword, and when it is held in the hand of someone adept at capturing your soul, no tool is stronger. A great novel brings you in, sits you down, and takes you down the path to self-reflection with the gentlest of hands. Isabel is one such writer.

Born on August 2, 1942, to Chilean parents in Peru, Isabel was primarily raised by the women in her family after her parents' divorce when she was a small child. She spent a great deal of time with her maternal grandmother, who was said to be a great storyteller and a driving inspiration to her. Before embarking on her journey as an author, she worked as a journalist and a broadcast interviewer before having to flee to Venezuela after her paternal uncle was assassinated in 1973.

But in 1981, a letter to her grandfather would change the course of her life and eventually plant the seeds for her first book, *The House of the Spirits*. subsequently became known as an author who seamlessly fuses magical realism, realistic fiction, fantasy, and myth. She followed up her 1982 debut with *The Porcelain Fat Lady* (1984), *Of Love and Shadows* (1985), and *Eva Luna* (1987). By 2025, she will have published twenty-eight books, been translated into over forty-two languages, and sold more than eighty million copies.

In addition to her passion for writing novels filled with the complexities of life, love, family, and womanhood, she is a passionate advocate for the empowerment and advancement of women and girls worldwide. A portion of her book sales is donated to the Isabel Allende Foundation, which she founded in honor of her late daughter Paula. Because of her advocacy work and her position as a feminist, she has garnered much acclaim worldwide for her stance on human rights.

In 2014, she was awarded the Presidential Medal of Freedom by President Barack Obama. In 2018, the National Book Foundation recognized her for its Medal for Distinguished Contribution to American Letters. Throughout her career, she has been recognized with over sixty awards in fifteen countries and has earned fifteen international honorary doctorates.

CRISTINA PERI ROSSI: THE VORACIOUS READER WHO DEFIED THE ODDS

Not everyone grows up knowing they want to be a writer. For many, their path to authorship is winding, eventually leading them where they need to go. As a child, Cristina knew what she wanted to do with her life and made sure that the people around her knew it. Her love of learning drove her passion for writing, as she would dissect various topics and genres in her fiction.

Born in Montevideo, Uruguay, on November 12, 1941, the renowned Latin American novelist knew that she would grow up to be a writer. She grew up reading and absorbing anything she could get her hands on, and quickly became a regular at the National Library in Montevideo. Cristina graduated with degrees in biology and comparative literature, and soon began teaching and writing her own material.

In 1963, she published her first book, *Viviendo: Relatos*, followed by *Los Museos Abandonados* in 1968, which won a young author award. Cristina's novels have become known for tackling themes like political and social injustices, love, sexuality, feminism, and gender.. Unfortunately, in 1972, she had to flee her home country due to mounting political repression and censorship at the hands of a military-led government.

Cristina relocated to Barcelona, where she continued to write articles and essays speaking out against the government in Uruguay. Her trenchant views led the regime to ban any mention of her or her literary works in the media. As a journalist for *Diario 16*, *El Periódico*, *Triunfo*, and *Agencia Efe*, she continually voiced her concerns and was forced into exile in France by the Franco dictatorship in 1974. Thankfully, her exile didn't last long, and by the end of that year, she was back in Spain.

Through the body of her work, the Uruguayan writer and novelist solidified herself as one of the many great Latin American authors who emerged out of the 1960s and 1970s. She has had her work translated into fifteen languages, won the Loewe International Poetry Prize in 2008, and been awarded the Cervantes Prize in 2021.

JULIA DE BURGOS: THE GRAND DAME OF AFRO-PUERTO RICAN LITERATURE

The trials and tribulations that authors and writers experience in life often become the palette with which they paint the world. It becomes the foundation for what they write about and how they go about articulating the themes that are in constant motion before their eyes. Julia's life was the backdrop for the stories and poems she painted:ones that danced with themes of feminism and social justice for Afro-Caribbeans.

Born February 17, 1914, in Santa Cruz in the Carolina province of Puerto Rico, she was the eldest of thirteen children (six of whom died in childhood). In 1928, she was awarded a scholarship to go to high school and eventually became a teacher after earning a degree from the University of Puerto Rico.

Unlike many light-skinned Afro-Puerto Ricans, Julia was had always been proud of her African heritage, a theme that appeared throughout many of her works. She was also a staunch supporter of Puerto Rican independence from the US and consistently advocated for anti-imperialist ideologies. In 1936, she joined the Nationalist Party of Puerto Rico after witnessing the despair of the Great Depression and experiencing frustration with the American occupation of the island.

While Julia went on to marry twice, she never strayed from her feminist ideals and added the "de" to her last name as a defiant act against the social norms of the time. Due to her beliefs, Julia often felt that she didn't fit into the intellectual circles of the time. The fact that she was a divorced woman and of African descent excluded her from social groups that weren't heavily focused on advancing women's rights or the civil rights of Afro-Puerto Ricans.

Julia published several poetic collections, such as *Poemas Exactos a mí Misma* (1937), *Poema en Veinte Surcos* (1938), and *Canción de la Verdad Sencilla* (1939). Many of her poems discussed the injustices that Indigenous people and enslaved Africans faced during the colonial period. In 1940, she decided to leave Puerto Rico behind and relocated to New York, where she met her partner, Juan Isidro Jimenez Grúllon.

Despite living in New York, she never stopped her activism or advocacy work on behalf of Puerto Rico, women, or the descendants of the enslaved Africans living on the island. Her literary works cemented her role as the mother of the 1960s Nuyorican movement in the United States. Unfortunately, suffering from health problems due to her bouts with alcoholism, she passed away on July 6, 1953, at the age of thirty-nine.

Her final collection, *El Mar y Tú*, was published posthumously by her sister in 1954. Since then, she has received awards from the Institute of Puerto Rican Literature and an honorary doctorate from the University of Puerto Rico. There are schools, parks, and cultural centers named after her, like the Julia de Burgos Cultural Arts Center in Cleveland, Ohio, the Julia de Burgos Latino Cultural Center in East Harlem, New York, and Julia de Burgos Park in Chicago, Illinois.

SOR JUANA INÉS DE LA CRUZ: THE ETERNAL LEARNER WHO WAS SILENCED

Women haven't always had the rights they have today. For centuries, women were relegated to caring for the home. What happened to the women who want to continue to learn unencumbered by the necessities of home life? They became nuns, as Sor Juana Inés did. As a child, she always showed a strong inclination for learning and writing, and reading was an enormous passion of hers.

While the year of her birth is highly debated, she was said to be born on November 12, 1648 or 1651, in San Miguel Nepantla in the Viceroyalty of New Spain (now Mexico). Sor Juana Inés was a woman with a lifelong passion for knowledge, but as a member of a family of modest means, formal schooling was not an option for her.

This didn't damp her thirst; it only made her more determined to teach herself as much as she could. By the time she was eight years old, she had written her first poem. By her teenage years, she was said to be well-versed in Greek logic, taught Latin to children, and had learned to speak, read, and write in the Aztecs' language, Nahuatl. Upon the death of her grandfather, she moved to Mexico City to live with her family, and it was there that people first started to hear about her advanced knowledge.

Because Sor Juana Inés wasn't interested in marriage, only in dedicating her life to study, she ultimately decided to join a convent. At her convent, she was able to have her own study and library where she would write, read about philosophy and the natural sciences, talk to scholars, and fill the room with maps and scientific instruments. In addition to teaching at a local school, she also served as the convent's archivist and accountant.

Sor Juana Inés went on to write plays, commissioned religious services, state addresses, and poetry, becoming known as one of the great writers of the Spanish Golden Age. The strength of her skill and her writing style also established her as the last great writer of the Hispanic Baroque period and the first great writer of colonial Mexican literature. Her work covered themes that were satirical, religious, moral, and secular. She even wrote some multilingual carols in Nahuatl, Hispano-African, and Spanish. The complete publication of her entire body of work runs to four volumes.

Her thirst for knowledge and desire to write about non-religious topics and themes brought much criticism from her political and religious superiors. Eventually, Sor Juana Inés was forced to stop writing as she had been. In 1695, a plague swept through the area, and she passed away on April 17 after having tended and cared for her fellow sisters.

DR. LORGIA GARCÍA PEÑA: *LA PROFE* WHO UNDERSTANDS THE IMPORTANCE OF LEARNING OUR HISTORY

The dynamics, foundations, and elements that went into establishing Latin America were molded into this imperfect statue that was then sold as perfection. Marginalized communities have historically borne the brunt of systemic oppression due to a lack of equity in the institutions that claim to have changed. Dr. Lorgia has spent a career diving deep into colonialism, antiblackness, xenophobia, and the erasure of Black, immigrant, and working communities.

Born in the Dominican Republic, *La Profe* moved to the United States when she was twelve and went on to earn an MA in Latin American and Latino Literatures from Rutgers University in New Jersey, and a PhD in American Culture from the University of Michigan. Through her work, she has highlighted the cultural, social, societal, and political contributions to the silencing of entire communities.

The Carnegie Corporation of New York quotes her as saying, "My path through academia has been shaped by my personal experiences as an immigrant, a woman of color, and a first-generation:the first person in my family to graduate from college. It is my radical hope that the work I do helps to shatter silences and to center the lives of the communities I come from and care for."

Her focus on Black Latinidades has led her to publish three books. *The Borders of Dominicanidad: Race, Nations, and Archives of Contradictions*, published in 2016, won the 2017 National Women's Studies Association Gloria E. Anzaldúa Book Prize, the 2016 LASA Latino/a Studies Book Award, and the 2016 Isis Duarte Book Prize in Haiti and Dominican Studies. It was also translated into Spanish in 2020.

Her 2022 book, *Translating Blackness: Latinx Colonialities in Global Perspective*, also won the Isis Duarte Book Prize in Haiti and Dominican Studies in 2023. Her third book, *Community as Rebellion*, was awarded the LASA Latinx Studies Award. Dr. Lorgia is also the co-founder of Freedom University Georgia, a school built on the premise of providing college-level instruction to undocumented students.

The effects of her work manifest widely, which is why *La Profe* has been recognized via awards throughout the years. The Massachusetts Institute of Technology (MIT) presented her with the Disobedience Award in 2017 for her outstanding work with Freedom University. In 2021, the Margaret Casey Foundation named her a Freedom Scholar, and in 2022 she received the Angela Davis Prize for Public Scholarship.

LOLA RODRÍGUEZ DE TIÓ: THE DREAMER OF A FREE PUERTO RICO

Freedom is a precious thing that is especially coveted when out of reach. The island of Puerto Rico has never known true sovereignty, so it's no surprise that so many of its inhabitants feel so strongly about its independence and autonomy. For Lola, a free Puerto Rico was all she ever wanted to experience in her life.

Born Dolores Rodríguez de Astudillo y Ponce de León on September 14, 1843, the Puerto Rican journalist, poet, and activist would become known for her outspoken criticisms of Spanish colonialism. Lola was born into an aristocratic family, which allowed her to further her studies and be surrounded by intellectuals of the time. She was married in 1865 to journalist Bonocio Tió Segarra, with whom she shared philosophies about Puerto Rico's sovereignty, at the age of twenty. In 1868, Lola wrote and completed her first major lyrical project, set to the tune of *"La Borinqueña"* (Puerto Rico's war cry denouncing Spanish rule), during the Grito de Lares revolt.

Lola's first book of poetry, *Mis Cantares*, was published in 1876 and sold about 2,500 copies. This poetry collection assured that she would be watched by the local Spanish officials from then on. Her opposing Spanish rule of Puerto Rico were so strong that she would go into exile three times over the course of her life. During her first exile, she was forced to flee to Venezuela in 1877, but eventually returned. Later, in 1887, she and her husband would again flee the country, going first to Venezuela and then Cuba.

While in Cuba, she published *Mi libro de Cuba* and continued her activism, which ultimately led to her exile once again. She and her husband relocated to New York City, where they helped José Martí and other Cuban revolutionaries with their cause. In 1899, she returned to Havana and remained there until her passing in November 1924.

Over the course of her life, she published twelve books and one song. She was best known for the lyrics to "*La Boriqueña*," *A mi Patria en la Muerte de Corchado* (1885), *Claros y Nieblas* (1885), and *Noche Buena* (1887).

CLORINDA MATTO DE TURNER: THE FIRST FEMALE FOUNDER OF A MAJOR NEWSPAPER IN LATIN AMERICA

We are a sum of all of our parts. As we develop into adulthood, the people, things, and situations we encounter become an integral part of who we are. It's in those moments that our humanity is formed. For Clorinda, growing up alongside Quechua-speaking communities in Peru proved to be her north star.

Born Grimanesa Martina Mato on November 11, 1852, Clorinda's love for writing would take her on a journey to become a highly respected novelist and journalist. Raised in Cuzco, and having lived on a hacienda in Calca, Clorinda spent a lot of time around the Indigenous communities of the area, developing a deep respect and love for them.

After marrying Joseph Turner in 1871, she resettled in the province of Canchis, where she further leaned into defending women's rights and speaking out against the exploitation of indigenous communities. In 1878, she founded and launched her magazine *El Recreo de Casco*, which discussed literature, art, education, and science, and also portrayed indigenous people in a positive light.

Throughout her career, she published six books, translated several Bible sections into Quechua, wrote a drama, and launched two publications. Of all her works, her most famous was *Aves Sin Nido*, which was about an indigenous woman and a white man falling in love, only to realize that they were the illegitimate children of a priest. Because of the controversial topics and themes she covered, she eventually left Peru for Argentina (where she passed away in 1901).

"We have to be visible. We are not ashamed of who we are."

SYLVIA RIVERA, AMERICAN GAY LIBERATION
AND TRANSGENDER RIGHTS ACTIVIST AND A
VETERAN OF THE 1969 STONEWALL INN
UPRISING

THREE
VOICES FOR CHANGE
FEMINISTS AND POLITICAL TRAILBLAZERS

We all know that progress doesn't just happen:it is demanded, crafted, and defended by those who dare to dream beyond the limits imposed on them. The women in this chapter were visionaries who refused to accept silencing, exclusion, or invisibility. They were feminists, educators, writers, journalists, and politicians who carved space for women in arenas long dominated by men. With pens, microphones, votes, and voices, they challenged governments, institutions, and traditions that sought to keep them in the shadows.

Some of these women sparked movements through education, insisting that knowledge was the foundation of equality. Others built feminist organizations, drafted petitions, and demanded reforms that shifted laws and minds. Journalists risked their safety to expose corruption and abuses of power, while political trailblazers broke barriers of race, gender, and sexuality to represent communities too often left behind.

Their methods varied:some radical, some cautious, some loud, some quiet:but all were united by a shared conviction: that women are not merely participants in history, but authors of it. They knew that fighting for equality required persistence, strategy, and courage.

As you read their stories, remember that change rarely comes without resistance. These women remind us that the fight for justice is not linear:it is built step by step, word by word, law by law, until entire systems are transformed. Their legacies are invitations: to raise your voice, to challenge injustice, and to believe that your actions, no matter how small, can ripple outward into movements that reshape nations.

DR. PAULINA LUISI: THE FEMINIST WHO PRESCRIBED JUSTICE

Paulina Luisi was a visionary who refused to stay in the lane assigned to her. She broke barriers in medicine, redefined what was possible for women in academia, and became one of Latin America's fiercest early feminists. As the first woman to earn a medical degree in Uruguay, she didn't just open doors:she kicked them wide open.

Born in 1875 in Argentina to European immigrant parents, Paulina moved to Uruguay as a child and grew up in a household that valued education and civic engagement. From a young age, she showed a sharp mind and relentless determination. She was the first woman in Uruguay to earn the equivalent of a bachelor's degree, and soon after enrolled in medical school:becoming the first woman to do so in a male-dominated institution that made no secret of its hostility toward her presence.

Medical school was more than challenging:it was hostile. Male classmates tried to intimidate her, ridicule her, and push her out. One infamous story claims someone placed a severed penis in the pocket of her lab coat. Without flinching, she held it up and calmly asked, "Did one of you lose this?" In that moment, Paulina didn't just stand her ground:she made it clear that she wasn't going anywhere.

After graduating in 1908, she specialized in gynecology and public health. But she didn't stop at clinical care:Paulina believed that real health meant fighting for systemic change. She advocated for sex education, reproductive rights, labor protections, and women's suffrage. In 1916, she founded and led the Uruguayan branch of the National Women's Council, which became a key driver in the push for gender equality across Latin America.

Her feminism was radical for its time:calling for legal equality between the sexes, questioning the institution of marriage, and demanding that women be seen as full political subjects. She fought to change laws, shift public opinion, and educate a new generation of women to fight for their rights.

When Uruguay granted women the right to vote in 1932, Paulina was working as a diplomat in Europe. Instead of staying abroad in a prestigious post, she resigned and returned home:believing that her country needed her on the ground more than in any embassy.

She also believed in the power of the media. After suffrage was won, she took to the airwaves, using radio to educate the public on feminist issues and political justice. By the early 1940s, she had become the female voice of Uruguay's Socialist Party and was affectionately known on the air as *La Abuela*:the grandmother of the movement.

Like many intellectuals of her time, she embraced some ideas:such as eugenics in public health:that are rightly condemned today. Her legacy is complex, but her contributions to feminist thought and social justice remain foundational.

Paulina Luisi died in 1950, but her impact lives on in Uruguay's progressive policies and in every Latina who refuses to be silenced or sidelined. She was more than the first woman doctor in her country:she was a force of nature, a strategist for equality, and a woman who knew that knowledge was power, and that power belonged in the hands of *mujeres*.

SARA JUSTO: THE EDUCATOR WHO PLANTED THE SEEDS OF FEMINISM IN ARGENTINA

Sara Justo was a woman of firsts:firsts that often went unnoticed, but quietly changed the course of Argentine feminism forever. A dentist by training and an educator by vocation, she became one of the earliest voices to link women's education, civic participation, and political rights in a country where women were still treated like legal minors.

Born in Buenos Aires in 1870, Sara was raised in a politically active but socially conservative family. While socialist ideas were not a major part of her early upbringing, her brother:Juan Bautista Justo, one of the founders of the Argentine Socialist Party:influenced her later shift toward feminist and social justice work.

Sara became one of Argentina's first female dentists, but her passion lay in education. She taught domestic economy and childcare to women and girls, using her classroom as a space not only to teach skills, but to plant the seeds of political awareness. As the director of the *Escuela Profesional de Mujeres Paula Albarracín de Sarmiento*, she was part of a movement that believed women deserved more than obedience and motherhood:they deserved knowledge, voice, and dignity.

But Sara was not content with the classroom. In 1905, alongside fellow pioneers Julieta Lanteri and Elvira Rawson, she co-founded the *Centro Feminista de la Argentina*:the country's first feminist organization. A year later, she was encouraged by Spanish feminist Belén de Sárraga to create a suffrage movement. By 1907, she helped form the *Comité Pro-Sufragio Femenino* with Alicia Moreau, aiming to promote "the intellectual, moral, and material emancipation of women, whatever their social conditions."

Sara didn't always agree with her peers on how to get there. While Alicia Moreau advocated for universal suffrage, Sara believed in a gradual approach:starting with local or municipal voting rights. She worried that many Argentine women lacked the education and political experience to wield full citizenship effectively in a patriarchal and deeply unequal society. Her caution wasn't hesitation:it was strategy.

Still, her activism was bold. In 1911, she helped draft a landmark petition on women's civil rights with Moreau, Rawson, and others, which Socialist congressman Alfredo Palacios presented to the Argentine legislature. That petition became the foundation for Argentina's 1926 Civil Rights Law for Women:one of the most significant feminist victories of the era.

Sara also traveled across Europe to study feminist movements first-hand, and brought her learnings back home. In 1909, she gave a groundbreaking lecture on European feminism and its lessons for Latin America. She argued that Argentine women needed unity, education, and patience:but also courage. "The majority of women," she said, "are still bound by fanaticism and lack the preparation to claim their rights consciously and intelligently."

Her vision of feminism was deeply rooted in education, maternal responsibility, and social reform. She believed that mothers were the first educators of future citizens:and if women were to shape a more just nation, they needed to be educated and politically aware themselves.

Unlike many of her peers, Sara never called for universal suffrage during her lifetime. But that didn't stop her from shaping the very infrastructure of feminist activism in Argentina. She participated in international congresses, published articles in major newspapers, and mentored the next generation of feminist leaders. Her quiet radicalism helped institutionalize feminism in Argentine civil society:without ever seeking the spotlight.

Sara Justo died in 1941, just six years before Argentine women finally won the right to vote. She didn't live to see it:but she helped build the road that led there. Her legacy reminds us that every movement needs thinkers and tacticians, not just firebrands. And sometimes, changing the world starts in the classroom.

NURIA PIERA: THE JOURNALIST WHO REFUSED TO STAY SILENT

Nuria Piera doesn't just report the news:she shakes the systems that try to bury it. For over three decades, this Dominican powerhouse has been at the forefront of investigative journalism in Latin America, fearlessly exposing corruption, impunity, and human rights abuses, often at great personal risk.

Born in Santo Domingo in 1960 to Spanish immigrant parents, Nuria's path toward truth-telling began with tragedy. When she was just eight years old, her father:Catalan journalist José Enrique Piera Puig:was assassinated during the authoritarian regime of Joaquín Balaguer. That loss forged her sense of justice and sharpened her resolve. What began as a child's grief became a lifelong mission: to speak for those silenced by fear, violence, and censorship.

Nuria began her television career early, but it was in 1987 that she truly changed the game with the launch of her investigative program

Nuria en el 9. It was the first of its kind in Dominican television:uncovering not only personal tragedies, but systemic failures. Week after week, she put herself on the line to expose scandals involving corruption, fraud, abuse, and cover-ups. But she didn't just point fingers:she demanded accountability.

One of her most explosive investigations came in 2013, when she revealed that the Vatican's former ambassador to the Dominican Republic, Józef Wesołowski, had been removed not over political disagreements, as the press claimed, but because of allegations of child sexual abuse. Her reporting helped bring to light yet another case of clerical pederasty, forcing global attention onto the Dominican Catholic Church and setting a precedent for confronting religious institutions with hard evidence.

Her work has earned her dozens of national and international awards, but it has also made her a target. In 2023, Amnesty International and Citizen Lab confirmed that Nuria's phone had been infected with Pegasus spyware multiple times between 2020 and 2021:a chilling example of state-level surveillance used to silence dissenting voices. She became the first confirmed journalist in the Dominican Republic targeted with military-grade spyware. Her crime? Investigating high-level corruption.

But Nuria refuses to back down. She has openly criticized digital platforms for spreading disinformation and harassment, calling them a *"cloaca"*:a cesspool:and has called for stronger regulation to protect journalists and democracy. She continues to stand in solidarity with other truth-tellers, like Edith Febles, Altagracia Salazar, and Huchi Lora, pushing back against smear campaigns and political blackmail with an unwavering voice.

Today, she serves as the CEO of NCDN (a news network she helped build through a joint venture between her company Provideo and CDN Canal 37), and remains one of the most respected journalists in the region. In 2014, she was named one of the most influential women in Ibero-America by EFE.

Nuria Piera's life is a testament to the power of journalism as a form of resistance. She didn't choose a safe path:but she chose a necessary one. And because of her, truth in the Dominican Republic has a name, a voice, and a face that refuses to disappear.

ANA IRMA RIVERA LASSÉN: THE TRAILBLAZER WHO TURNED RESISTANCE INTO REPRESENTATION

Ana Irma Rivera Lassén has never waited for permission to lead:she's carved her own path and opened the door for others to follow. An Afro-Puerto Rican feminist, lawyer, and human rights defender, she made history as the first Black and openly lesbian woman to run for Resident Commissioner of Puerto Rico in 2024. Her candidacy didn't just challenge the colonial status quo:it redefined what political power in Puerto Rico could look like.

Born in Santurce in 1955 to two educators, Rivera Lassén was raised with a deep sense of justice, curiosity, and civic responsibility. After earning degrees in humanities and law from the University of Puerto Rico, she became known for fighting gender-based discrimination in the legal system. In the 1980s, she successfully challenged court dress codes that unfairly targeted women:an early sign of her commitment to dismantling institutional bias.

Her list of firsts is long. In 2012, she became the first Afro-Puerto Rican and open lesbian to lead the Puerto Rico Bar Association. Under her leadership, the institution advanced gender equality, LGBTQ+ rights, and access to justice:especially for people historically excluded from legal protections. A decade later, she brought the same energy to electoral politics as a co-founder of the Citizen Victory Movement (MVC), winning a Senate seat in 2020 and using her platform to fight for reproductive rights, climate justice, and anti-corruption reforms.

By 2024, Rivera Lassén was back on the ballot:this time running for Resident Commissioner in Washington, DC as part of the *Alianza de País*, a historic coalition between the MVC and the Puerto Rican Independence Party. Although she placed third, the campaign was groundbreaking: It elevated a Black, queer feminist to one of the island's most high-profile races and helped push the *Alianza* to become Puerto Rico's second-ranked political force.

Her candidacy was unapologetically intersectional. Rivera Lassén never hid who she was:she centered it. She spoke openly about her identities, her decades-long relationship with her wife, sociologist Elizabeth Crespo Kebler, and her lifelong commitment to social justice. She also pushed for policies that held governments accountable, including creating public tools to track the use of federal funds and calling out entrenched political corruption.

Despite facing a flood of structural bias:including racism, homophobia, and misinformation:Rivera Lassén remained focused on the bigger picture. She knew her campaign was part of a longer struggle for dignity and inclusion, and saw her work as laying the groundwork for the next generation of leaders.

Though the *Alianza* didn't win the majority of seats, it broke the long-standing two-party system and reshaped political discourse on the island. Rivera Lassén called on her coalition to embrace its new role as a strong, organized opposition:ready to hold power accountable, defend human rights, and continue building a more just Puerto Rico.

Her life and career are reminders that progress is not just about visibility:it's about building movements that last. With every barrier she's broken, Ana Irma Rivera Lassén has redefined what leadership looks like in Puerto Rico:and shown that resistance, when grounded in love and community, becomes transformation.

ARGELIA LAYA: THE REVOLUTIONARY EDUCATOR WHO FOUGHT WITH HER VOICE:AND HER FISTS

Argelia Laya didn't just challenge the system:she fought it from every angle: as an educator, guerrilla fighter, feminist organizer, congresswoman, and unapologetic Black woman from Venezuela. For more than five decades, she wove grassroots activism and radical politics into every part of her life, becoming one of the most influential feminists in Latin American history.

Born in 1926 in Barlovento, a coastal region rich in Afro-Venezuelan culture, Argelia was raised by politically active parents who instilled in her a deep sense of justice and pride in her African roots. Her mother was part of the Women's Cultural Assembly, and her father was a guerrilla fighter who resisted dictatorship in the 1930s. After political persecution forced the family into poverty on the outskirts of Caracas, Argelia began to understand how class, race, and gender oppression intersect:and how they require collective resistance.

By nineteen, she had earned a teaching degree, and shortly after, her personal and political lives collided. After surviving a sexual assault and becoming pregnant, she faced dismissal from her teaching post due to a law banning unmarried mothers from working in education. Rather than accept injustice, Argelia wrote a letter to the Minister of Education, invoking constitutional protections for maternity. She won her case and was transferred to a rural school, where she launched an adult literacy campaign:turning punishment into purpose.

This moment sparked a lifelong fight for reproductive justice and the rights of working-class women. Argelia was one of the first

Venezuelan women to speak publicly about the need to decriminalize abortion and defend women's right to raise children without state or employer punishment. She campaigned for gender equality in education, workplace protections, and an end to violence against women. Long before the word "intersectionality" existed, Argelia lived it:naming how sexism, racism, and poverty combined to oppress Afro-descendant and Indigenous women most of all.

But she didn't stop at advocacy. In the 1950s, Argelia joined the Communist Party of Venezuela and helped organize resistance against the Marcos Pérez Jiménez dictatorship. When the party went underground and embraced armed struggle, she took the name "Commander Jacinta" and joined the guerrilla movement. There, she insisted on equal political roles for women and confronted the misogyny within her own revolutionary circles.

After leaving the armed struggle in 1964, she returned to politics, serving multiple terms in Venezuela's National Assembly and co-founding the Movement to Socialism (MAS). In 1991, she became the first woman to lead a major political party in Venezuela. She also helped found the country's first organization of Black women and worked to reform civil, labor, and suffrage laws:fighting for maternity leave, childcare, sex ed in schools, and protections for young mothers to continue their education.

Argelia's political vision was clear: Women's liberation was inseparable from socialism. She argued that capitalism thrived on sexism and that full equality could only be achieved in a system that dismantled both patriarchy and class exploitation. Her activism reflected that belief:whether leading feminist assemblies, debating in Parliament, or walking into a guerrilla camp.

Argelia passed away in 1997, just months before the Bolivarian Revolution began:a movement she had helped make possible through decades of grassroots organizing. Today, her name lives on through the Argelia Laya Feminist School Foundation, a new generation of

Afro-feminists, and the ongoing struggle for abortion rights and racial justice across Venezuela.

Argelia Laya taught us that feminism is not just about identity:it's about transformation and being an integral part of building the future.

CLORINDA MATTO DE TURNER: THE NOVELIST WHO CHALLENGED THE NATION

Clorinda Matto de Turner was a literary trailblazer whose bold pen took aim at racism, patriarchy, and colonial arrogance in nineteenth-century Peru. Although she came from an elite landowning background, she used her privilege to challenge systems of oppression and advocate for Indigenous rights, women's education, and cultural reform.

Born Grimanesa Martina Mato in Cuzco:the heart of the former Inca Empire:she was raised on her father's hacienda, where she grew up speaking Quechua and engaging deeply with the traditions and realities of Indigenous life. This early exposure shaped her worldview and later inspired her most powerful work. As a young woman, she studied subjects far beyond what was considered acceptable for women at the time:including philosophy and natural science:and later began publishing under the name Clorinda, inspired by a warrior woman in Italian literature.

After the death of her husband left her in debt, she rebuilt her life through journalism, education, and activism. She became the first woman in the Americas to edit a major daily newspaper, and she founded her own press, staffed by women. She also launched *Los Andes*, a magazine dedicated to women's issues and national reform.

Her groundbreaking novel *Aves sin Nido* (*Birds Without a Nest*), published in 1889, shook Peru to its core. It depicted the cruel realities of Indigenous communities exploited by corrupt landowners and priests. The novel was so controversial that the Catholic Church excommunicated her, and mobs burned her books in the streets. But the attention only solidified her status as one of Peru's most daring thinkers.

Matto de Turner was a central figure in the *indigenismo* movement:a group of mostly non-Indigenous writers and intellectuals who sought to center Indigenous people and cultures in the national conscious-ness. While not Indigenous herself, she fiercely advocated for their inclusion in education, citizenship, and national progress, arguing that Peru's future depended on embracing both its Indigenous and European roots.

After her exile to Argentina during political unrest in 1895, she continued to write, teach, and publish. She even translated the Gospels into Quechua and founded *El Búcaro Americano*, a family magazine focused on education and social issues. She died in Buenos Aires in 1909, far from home:but in 1924, her body was returned to Peru and reburied with honors.

Clorinda Matto de Turner helped redefine what it meant to be a woman of letters in Latin America. Through literature, she demanded a more inclusive nation:one where women and Indige-nous peoples could live with dignity, education, and equality. Though not of Indigenous descent herself, her commitment to ampli-fying their voices changed the literary and political landscape of Latin America forever.

MARGARITA MBYWANGI: FROM ENSLAVED CHILD TO INDIGENOUS LEADER

Margarita Mbywangi's life is proof that even the most painful begin-nings can give rise to extraordinary leadership. Born in 1962 in the forests of Canindeyú, Paraguay, to an Aché family of hunters, her childhood was violently cut short. At just five years old, she was captured by Paraguayan settlers and sold into forced domestic labor:a practice that stripped countless Aché children from their lands during the Stroessner dictatorship.

Passed between wealthy ranching families, Margarita grew up not as a daughter, but as a servant. She wore hand-me-down clothes, cared for other people's children, and longed for the love she was denied. One of her "sisters," a teacher, managed to get her into school, where she learned Spanish and basic literacy. But without a birth certificate, her education stalled. By her teenage years, she began dreaming of escape.

At sixteen, Margarita tried to flee, but was caught and dragged back. Two years later, she succeeded:moving to Ciudad del Este to work as a domestic helper. With the help of a priest, she eventually traced members of her biological family. At age twenty, she returned to the Aché community, though she no longer spoke her language and felt like a stranger among her own people. The adjustment was brutal; she battled isolation and alcoholism before slowly reclaiming her heritage.

Determined to heal and contribute, Margarita trained as a nurse and began working for her community. Over time, she became a respected leader, and was elected cacique of Kuetuvy, where she guided forty families. Her activism deepened in the 1980s and 1990s as she fought illegal logging and defended Indigenous land rights, efforts that led to both political recognition and imprisonment.

Her leadership reached a historic milestone in 2008, when President Fernando Lugo appointed her Minister of Indigenous Affairs:the first Indigenous person in Paraguay ever to hold a cabinet position. Though her appointment was met with resistance, even from some Indigenous groups, Margarita vowed to serve all communities equally. She pushed for legalizing Indigenous land titles and protecting forests, which she described as "our mother, our life, our present, and future."

Beyond politics, Margarita has been a voice for truth. Through blogs, interviews, and speeches, she has shared her personal story of survival and resilience, reminding the world of the injustices faced by the Aché and the strength it takes to reclaim stolen identity.

Today, Margarita Mbywangi stands as a symbol of endurance and dignity. From enslaved child to national leader, her journey embodies both the wounds and the resilience of Paraguay's Indigenous peoples:and the unbreakable spirit of a woman who refused to be silenced.

PRUDENCIA AYALA: THE PRESIDENTIAL CANDIDATE WHO WAS BRAVE ENOUGH TO BE FIRST

Prudencia Ayala refused to accept the limits placed on her because of her gender, race, or class. In 1930, at a time when Salvadoran women were not even allowed to vote, she declared her candidacy for president. Her bold campaign:rooted in honesty, workers' rights, and equality:made her the first woman in Latin America to seek the highest political office.

Born in 1885 in Sonsonate, El Salvador, Prudencia was of Indigenous and African descent and grew up in a working-class household. She left school after the second grade, but never stopped teaching herself. A seamstress by trade, she became a writer, poet, and outspoken critic of injustice. Through articles, books, and eventually her own newspaper, *Redención Femenina*, she raised her voice against imperialism, corruption, and the exclusion of women from public life.

Her outspokenness was risky. She was jailed more than once for her political writings and activism, but prison never silenced her. Instead, it strengthened her resolve. In her work, she argued that women deserved full citizenship:not only as mothers or caretakers, but as active participants in the nation's political future.

When Prudencia announced her run for the presidency under the Unionist Party, her platform was groundbreaking. She called for workers' rights, transparency in government, access to education, limits on alcohol, respect for freedom of worship, and recognition of children born outside of marriage. Most radical of all, she demanded suffrage and political equality for women.

The Supreme Court ultimately rejected her candidacy, ruling that women were not recognized as "citizens." Her campaign ended before it truly began, but the impact was seismic. Prudencia had claimed space that no woman before her had dared to occupy. She proved that political leadership was not the sole domain of men, even in a society determined to deny women the vote.

Ridiculed as *"Prudencia, la loca"* by detractors, she was mocked for her Indigenous features, her gender, and her audacity. Yet her vision was clear: Democracy without women was no democracy at all.

Prudencia Ayala died in 1936, years before Salvadoran women gained the right to vote in 1950. For decades, she was erased from official history, but feminist movements have since reclaimed her as a symbol of courage and defiance. In 2017, a street in San Salvador was named Avenida Prudencia Ayala in her honor.

Her legacy endures as proof that daring to step forward, even when the odds are stacked against you, can change the course of history.

ALEXANDRIA OCASIO-CORTEZ:THE YOUNGEST EVER TO DO IT

Our communities are everything to us. We want to see them flourish, feel safe, and know that they are protected from harm. No one could have predicted the monumental changing of tides that Alexandria pulled off in 2018 when she beat nineteen-year incumbent Joseph Crowley for New York's 14th congressional district. This win made her the youngest women ever to serve in the United States Congress.

Alexandria was born on October 13, 1989, in the Bronx borough of New York City, to a Puerto Rican mother and a Bronx-born father. While she went on to pursue a career in politics, one of her childhood passions was science. In 2007, the Latina politician won second place in microbiology at the Intel International Science and Engineering Fair. MIT's Lincoln Laboratory honored her by naming an asteroid after her.

She went on to graduate cum laude from Boston University in 2011 with a bachelor's degree in international relations and economics. While a student there, she interned for US Senator Ted Kennedy's immigration office. Upon graduation, she returned to New York City and worked as a bartender and waitress to supplement her mother's income. During this time, she established a publishing company which specialized in children's literature and sought to portray the Bronx in a more positive light.

Despite having worked as a campaign organizer for Bernie Sanders's presidential campaign in 2016, Alexandria still thought that running for a political seat was out of reach for her. It wasn't until a visit to the Dakota Access Pipeline protest at the Standing Rock Sioux Reservation in 2016 that she finally saw what could be possible for her.

When she began her bid against Joseph Crowley, she knew the odds be against her, but she grounded herself in one simple principle: She wanted what was best for her community. She went on to beat the Democratic incumbent 57% to 42% in the primary elections. Come the general elections, up against Republican nominee Tina Forte, she won 69.2% to 30.8%.

Alexandria's Congressional wins since then have proven what is possible when you lead with heart and spur yourself on fearlessly.

SONIA SOTOMAYOR: THE BRONX *PUERTORRIQUEÑA* WHO BECAME A LEGAL TORCHBEARER

Our fearless belief in ourselves is oftentimes what helps us reach insurmountable heights. Whether in our personal lives or within the legal system, knowing that everything you need to succeed is already inside of you is a must. Sonia, the first Latina and third woman sworn in as a United States Supreme Court Justice, understood this simple philosophy from an early age.

The Latina changemaker was born on June 25, 1954, in the Bronx, New York, to Puerto Rican natives Juan Sotomayor, a manual laborer, and Celina Baez, a nurse. By the time she was seven, Sonia had been diagnosed with diabetes, and soon learned how to sterilize her needles and self-administer her insulin. This is said to be when she learned the important lesson of self-reliance and how to push yourself forward despite your circumstances.

As a child, she enjoyed reading Nancy Drew mystery books, but it wasn't until she watched the 1957 legal drama *Perry Mason* that she took an interest in becoming a lawyer. From that moment on, she set her sights on pursuing a legal career. Sonia graduated from high school as a valedictorian and earned a scholarship to Princeton University. While there, she served as the co-chairman of the activist group *Acción Puertorriqueña*, where she accused the Princeton administration of discriminating against Puerto Ricans in hiring.

In 1976, she graduated summa cum laude with a bachelor's degree in history, and went on to attend Yale Law School for her juris doctor (JD). As a student, she co-chaired the Latin American and Native American Students Association, was the editor for *The Yale Law Journal*, and published an article on Puerto Rico's right to offshore minerals. Following her graduation from Yale, she went to work at the Manhattan district attorney's office under Robert Morgenthau.

Through her work there, Sonia established herself as a legal mind with a backbone and prosecuted everything from petty crimes to homicides. In 1984, she moved to a private firm, Pavia & Harcourt, working in business and corporate law with a focus on intellectual property rights and copyright litigation. She eventually became partner in 1988.

In November 1991, the George H. W. Bush administration nominated Sonia to the United States District Court for the Southern District of New York. There she gained some fame due to her ruling in the *Silverman v. Major League Baseball Player Relations Committee, Inc.* case which brought her renown as the judge who "saved" baseball.

In 1997, the Clinton administration nominated her to the United States Court of Appeals for the Second Circuit, where she heard over three thousand cases and wrote about 380 majority opinions. Her work spoke for itself, something that led the Obama administration to appoint her as the replacement for Justice David Souter, who was retiring from the High Court.

"Peace cannot exist without justice, justice cannot exist without fairness, fairness cannot exist without development, development cannot exist without democracy, democracy cannot exist without respect for the identity and worth of cultures and peoples."

RIGOBERTA MENCHÚ TUM, K'ICHE'
GUATEMALAN HUMAN RIGHTS ACTIVIST,
FEMINIST, AND NOBEL PEACE PRIZE
LAUREATE.

FOUR
MINDS OF DISCOVERY
PIONEERS OF SCIENCE AND TECHNOLOGY

If there is one thing that holds true, it's that science and technology have taught us to dream about making the impossible possible. It has taken us to the moon, developed cures for illnesses once thought incurable, and made it possible to interact with your *familia* in the country of your heritage and ancestry from a comfortable couch miles away. The marvels of today's society are things future descendants will see as the norm.

Science and technology have also taught us that to live and survive, we need to continue to create, expand, adapt, and evolve. Sometimes, that change is met with resistance, but to resist is foolhardy and futile. They say that the future is female, but as it stands, the future is multifaceted, and women will be at the forefront of it, as they have always been.

The women in this chapter have crossed barriers, borders, and atmospheres, and fought to ensure that the *hermanas*, *amigas*, and women they will never meet get the chance to push scientific and technological advances that much further. The future is female, but more specifically, it's Latina.

NICOLE AUIL-GOMEZ: THE ECO-WARRIOR AND VOICE OF MOTHER EARTH

The *pachamama* gives us life, and in return, our task is to protect her from harm. While the rapid growth of society has made that difficult at times, conservationists haven't shied away from the often complex journey ahead of them. From the moment she began her career in 1996, Nicole has been a dedicated advocate for the planet she loves.

Born in Belize, she understood the importance of protecting the ecosystems that harmoniously work to provide us with air, sustenance, and more. Throughout Nicole's career, she has championed the use of nature-based and science-backed solutions to help societies adapt to climate change, and supported policy-making to promote sustainable fisheries. She has passionately spoken out against wildlife trafficking and the trading of endangered species.

The World Wildlife Fund quotes her as saying, "Science is important, as it provides evidence needed to make or advocate for informed decision-making. In the field of conservation, this would be in the best interest of the natural world, while not harming people."

Over the twenty-five-plus years of her career, she has contributed and published several scientific papers, all sharing research targeting the mortality of the endangered Antillean manatee, as well as how to protect these animals and the ecosystem they live in. As Country Director for the Wildlife Conservation Society (WCS) in Belize, she has supported initiatives that encourage biodiversity assessments and the management and expansion of marine protected areas.

In addition to her position at the WCS, Nicole has also been the executive director of the MPA-managing NGO Southern Environmental Association, as well as the Mesoamerican Region co-chairperson for the IUCN SSC Sirenian Specialist Group.

SABRINA GONZALEZ PASTERSKI: THE GENIUS REVOLUTIONIZING HOW WE SEE THE UNIVERSE

In past decades and centuries, it was believed that women wouldn't fare well in "harder" topics like science, technology, engineering, and math (STEM) because they had a more "delicate" constitution. That has never been the case, and Sabrina is a prime example of the genius that lies within women.

Born June 3, 1993, in Chicago, Illinois, Sabrina has been quoted as having called herself a proud "first-generation Cuban-American" and proud alumna of the Chicago public school system. Called the "Next Albert Einstein," by the time she was sixteen, she had already taken flying lessons and built and flown her own single-engine airplane from a kit.

Her genius has earned her a bachelor's degree in physics from the Massachusetts Institute of Technology (MIT), where she graduated with a 5.0 GPA. Because of her exceptional work at MIT, she was the first woman to graduate No. 1 in her class in the MIT Physics program. She proceeded to Harvard for her doctorate, and there, she, her colleagues, and her professor Andrew Strominger discovered the spin memory effect.

This discovery enables scientists to study the "fingerprint" left behind by gravitational waves across the fabric of space-time itself. She was also able to complete a solo paper on the Pasterski–Strominger–Zhiboedov triangle. This theory seeks to explain and find the connections between space symmetries, memory effects, and particle behavior (think of it as three separate trails in a forest that all lead to a hidden mountain). Her findings in this paper were cited by Stephen Hawking in one of his papers in 2016.

Within months of completing her doctorate at Harvard, she founded the Celestial Holography Initiative (CHI). The goal of the initiative is to gain a deeper understanding of how the universe records the lasting effects of cosmic events over time. It also seeks to uncover any hidden patterns that could link gravity to quantum physics.

Deeply understanding the difference female energy can make within STEM, Sabrina has used her platform to advocate for more inclusive and equitable programs for girls and women.

KATYA ECHAZARRETA: THE ONE WHO REACHED FOR THE STARS

People say that space is the final frontier, and the last thing to explore in the universe. For many women, space exploration feels like something unattainable due to the internalized belief that the sciences are difficult to understand. Katya has proven that Latinas can excel in the STEM fields and reach for the stars.

Born in Guadalajara, Mexico, on June 15, 1995, Katya moved to the United States when she was eight years old, something she has said was difficult due to the language barrier. Despite all the challenges she faced in those early years, she became fluent in English within two years of moving to California.

The spirited Latina went on to earn her bachelor's degree in electrical engineering from UCLA. While there, she applied to the

NASA Jet Propulsion Laboratory's internship program, which provided the launch pad for her full-time engineering career at the space agency. While working at NASA, she worked on five missions, including the Perseverance Mars rover and the Europa Clipper.

Despite having worked on several space projects for the agency, her most memorable experience was participating in the Space for Humanity initiative in June 2022. Kayta beat out over seven thousand applicants from more than 120 countries and became one of six individuals elected by the initiative to fly into space on the Blue Origin NS-21 flight as a Space for Humanity Ambassador. This established her as the first Mexican woman to go into space, following in the footsteps of Rodolfo Neri Vela, who became the first Mexican man to travel off Earth in 1985.

Since then, Katya has used her platform to demonstrate to young girls that engineering and the sciences are subjects in which they can excel. Now, she mentors women who are pursuing their passion for STEM and helps them navigate the field. She also established her own foundation, *Fundación Espacial*, which provides free admission to space camp to children in Mexico.

DR. LYA IMBER DE CORONIL: *LA QUE SALVÓ A LOS NIÑOS*

Latinas are molded by the uniqueness of their environments. While some are born into their home countries, others find themselves immigrants in a new land they will call their own. For Dr. Lya, Venezuela would be the country that held her heart.

Born in Ukraine on March 17, 1914, she found herself relocating with her family at the age of sixteen to the South American country in 1930. She soon began her medical studies at the Central University of Venezuela and became the first woman in the country to do so. As her focus was on the health and development of children, she subsequently became the first female pediatrician.

Dr. Lya went on to dedicate her entire career to serving, protecting, and advocating for the health and wellness of children in Venezuela. This led her to become one of the founders of the Venezuelan Society of Childcare and Pediatrics, where she served as both treasurer and president.

She was also on the board of UNICEF as vice president, where she addressed the correlation between equal and equitable access to financial opportunities, and health and disease dynamics. In an interview with her younger sister, Sofía Imber, in the 1980s, she discussed how the socioeconomic factors of the family unit directly affected the health of the children.

Dr. Lya asserted in the interview, "After having said it many times, and having repeated myself many times, it is clear that socioeconomic and cultural dynamics have a distinct effect on the lives of children. I don't think we can waste time, because this is a fact that has been universally agreed upon."

She went on to publish several scientific papers on the topic. Dr. Lya also held several other top positions within the field, such as director of the J. M. de los Ríos Children's Hospital in Caracas. She also became the first woman to serve on the Board of Directors of the College of Physicians of the Federal District.

She passed away in Venezuela in September 1981, leaving behind a legacy of medical advancements in children's health.

ANA KAREN RAMÍREZ TELLEZ: THE EPIC STEM QUEEN PAVING THE WAY *PARA LAS DEMÁS*

Society has made it so that generations of women believed that studying subjects such as science, technology, engineering, and mathematics was out of reach. This belief ultimately discouraged women from pursuing rewarding and engaging careers within these fields, which has led to low numbers of women in STEM, especially Latinas. Thankfully, future generations will have Ana Karen's advocacy work to thank for helping break down the imaginary barriers that keep women out.

The STEM entrepreneur, from Morelia in the Michoacán province of Mexico, has worked tirelessly to promote the development of technical skills, enabling young girls to feel confident in achieving their dreams and goals. Since 2015, her company, Epic Queen, has hosted online boot camps, mentoring programs, "hackathons," and gatherings for girls who show an interest in the STEM fields.

Ana Karen's goal to close the gender gap in STEM has led her to impact over seventy thousand girls across Latin America by creating a safe space for them to learn, explore, and express themselves.

The enterprising Latina shared with the EGADE Business School, "We have created safe learning spaces where thousands of women dare to dream of a future in STEM, overcoming barriers and generating innovative solutions."

Not only has her work helped encourage young girls to discover their STEM potential, she is also helping to create more qualified professionals for the industry as a whole. In 2020, she told *MIT Technology Review* that "there are more than twenty million jobs related to STEM," with not enough people graduating to cover the demand.

Due to her advocacy and life's mission, she has been internationally recognized for her work. She has received the EXATEC EGADE Merit Award (2019), *MIT Technology Review*'s Innovators Under 35 (2020), and Women in Tech Global Award (2023). The Association of Mexican Entrepreneurs (ASEM) also acknowledged Ana Karen among the top 100 entrepreneurs of Mexico.

ADELAIDA CHAVERRI-POLINI: THE STAUNCH DEFENDER OF THE GREEN

Nature is humanity's most significant gift from the universe. A great deal can be derived from it, including sustenance, medicine, and environmental protection. As populations have grown, an increasing number of forests and natural habitats have been affected by deforestation and climate change. This is something that Adelaida spent an entire career working to reverse.

The tropical forest and conservationist was born in Costa Rica on May 21, 1947, and began her career after studying both mathematics and biology at the University of Costa Rica. In the 1970s, she helped establish the Costa Rican Nature Conservation Association to help raise awareness of the importance of protecting local biodiversity and ecosystems. The primary focus of her work was tropical forests and marshes.

Her tireless work also led her and her colleagues to convince the government to establish both the Chirripó National Park and the Corcovado National Park (which expanded the country's national park service). Over the years, Adelaida became a leading expert on the Chirripó National Park, and even wrote a book on it, *Historia Natural del Parque Nacional Chirripó*.

Looking to ensure that she passed on her knowledge and love of conservation to future generations, she became a lecturer at the School of Environmental Sciences at the Universidad Nacional in Costa Rica. Adelaida was also a co-founder of the Monteverde Cloud Forest Preserve, which is run by the Tropical Science Center, and it remains a highly studied phenomenon.

Along with her numerous scientific publications, her work led to her being regarded and recognized as one of the world's leading experts on the conservation of forests and marshes. Some of her work even contributed to the discovery of new fungus species. Adelaida passed away in September 2003, leaving behind a legacy of conservation and a body of work that forever changed how Costa Rica approaches the protection of its forests.

In 2020, a special stamp was released to honor her contributions to her home country for International Women's Day.

MATILDE HIDALGO NAVARRO DE PRÓCEL: *LA NIÑA QUE PUDO*

It isn't just anyone who can make history and change society's internalized limiting beliefs about what is possible. Typically, it takes someone with vision and purpose, who can see the long-lasting and widespread effects of their dreams. Mathilde was one of those women who understand that they don't need to fall in line with what others do or say just because that is what was always done.

Born in Loja, Ecuador, on September 29, 1889, Matilde was one of six children born to a seamstress. Like many exceptional Latinas, she demonstrated a special aptitude for her studies from a young age. Upon finishing sixth grade, she dreamed of continuing to high school, something that came true despite being riddled with much strife, as some people in her community ostracized her.

Undeterred by the treatment she received from her peers, she excelled, and on October 8, 1913, she became the first woman to graduate from high school in Ecuador. Now, with the education bug deeply planted in her heart, she continued her education by pursuing a career in medicine. That journey wasn't without its troubles, as the dean of the faculty of the medical school near her refused to admit her.

Not one to take no for an answer, she enrolled at the University of Azuay in 1919 and went on to graduate with a medical degree, earning honors. In 1921, she returned to Quito and enrolled in the

Central University of Ecuador to complete her doctorate. Upon graduating, she became the first woman in Ecuador to earn a doctorate.

Like many spitfires, Matilde didn't stop with her education and medical degrees; she also challenged the status quo further by announcing that she would be voting in the 1924 presidential elections. After much deliberation from within the government, she was allowed to vote. On June 9, 1924, she became the first woman to cast a vote in a national election in Latin America. This moment in history also marked Ecuador as the first country on the continent to allow women to vote.

Matilde also became the first female vice president of her local municipality's council and the first deputy elected to Congress. She was awarded the National Merit Award in 1956 and 1971 by both the president and the minister of public health of Ecuador.

The enterprising Latina was the founding member of both the Medical Federation of Ecuador and the Surgical Association of Quito. The Ecuadorian Red Cross granted her the esteemed title of Honorary Lifetime President in the El Oro province. After she died in 1974, her hometown of Loja established a museum in her honor, and she was awarded the Medal of Merit and the Medal of Public Health by governmental decree.

DR. ELMA KAY: *LA AVENTURERA* WHO WANTED TO SAVE THE WORLD

There is so much that nature can teach us if we just listen to the whispers that ride on the waves of the wind. If taken seriously, it can help us unlock secrets of the world around us and drive us to a deeper understanding of ourselves. For Elma, growing up surrounded by lush green forests proved to be the defining element that would light the path of her life's work.

Born in Corozal, Belize, the conservationist explains how being around the flora and fauna of her local community sparked her curiosity to explore nature and live a truly outdoorsy life. Her love for examining nature and her local ecosystems sparked her scientific curiosity. She has publicly shared that "going to do science" was something she had "no doubt" she would end up doing.

Elma earned a scholarship to St. John's Junior College in Belize City. She later attended Saint Louis University. Her early career saw her embarking on a journey that would take her far away from her home country, but would prove to be incredibly rewarding and valuable. She was able to work across the Caribbean in Jamaica, Puerto Rico, Cuba, and the Dominican Republic.

After completing her master's degree, a meeting with Sharon Matola led to her course-correcting and returning to Belize. Alongside Sharon, she worked to launch the Belize Zoo and Tropical Education Center, with Elma establishing the botanical gardens and collection at the zoo.

Being back in Belize allowed her to utilize all the things she had learned during her many years abroad and apply them to her work locally. Elma co-founded the Environmental Research Institute at the University of Belize. She is also the managing director of the Belize Maya Forest Trust, a non-governmental organization that manages the Belize Maya Forest.

Throughout her career, she has been an advocate on topics such as climate change and policies that encourage conservation and the protection of wild plant and animal species.

DR. ELLEN OCHOA: THE LITTLE GIRL WHO SAW HERSELF AMONG THE STARS

Space travel is something many people dream of, but only few get to achieve. For Ellen, her dream of being among the stars was something she never gave up on. Her tenacity, grit, and belief in herself saw her embark on four trips into space and become the first Latina in space.

Born on May 10, 1958, in Los Angeles, California, the trailblazing astronaut was the middle child of five children to a Mexican-American father. Due to the discrimination he experienced as a child speaking Spanish, Ellen's father made the conscious decision not to teach his children to speak the language, in an effort to protect them.

Growing up, it is said that Ellen excelled at school and graduated from high school as her class valedictorian. She went on to earn a bachelor's degree in physics from San Diego University and a master's degree and doctorate in electrical engineering from Stanford University. Ellen went on to co-establish three new systems, all of which received patents, one of which included an optical system that helped detect imperfections in repeating patterns.

Ellen had been rejected twice from entry to the National Aeronautics and Space Administration's (NASA) Astronaut Training Program before she was accepted on her third try in 1990. By July 11, 1991, she had successfully completed the program and officially become an astronaut. Her first space mission was on April 8, 1993, where she and her fellow crew members spent nine days aboard the space shuttle Discovery, researching the effects of the sun on Earth's environment.

Her second mission came in November 1994, where she spent eight days studying ozone layer damage. A year after giving birth to her first child in 1998, she embarked on her third trip to space, whose mission saw her dock a spacecraft onto the International Space Station (ISS). Ellen's final space mission was in 2002, after giving birth to another child. She logged a total of 978 hours in space.

In 2013, she became the first Johnson Space Center director of Latino/Latine descent. She was also the second woman to hold the position. Ellen has received several accolades and awards for her work, including NASA's Distinguished Service Medal, Exceptional Service Medal, Outstanding Leadership Medal, and four Space Flight Medals.

She has received the Harvard Foundation Science Award, Women in Aerospace Outstanding Achievement Award, the Hispanic Engineer Albert Baez Award for Outstanding Technical Contribution to Humanity, the Hispanic Heritage Leadership Award, and San Diego State University Alumna of the Year (1995). On September 15, 2025, Mattel released a Dr. Ellen Ochoa Barbie to celebrate Hispanic Heritage Month.

"The Latina in me is an ember that blazes forever."

SONIA SOTOMAYOR, FIRST LATINA UNITED STATES SUPREME COURT ASSOCIATE JUSTICE

FIVE

GUARDIANS OF CULTURE

MUSICIANS, ARTISTS, AND CREATIVES

Throughout history, women artists have faced exclusion, censorship, and invisibility. Their talents were dismissed as hobbies, their identities erased from paintings, concert halls, and film reels. Yet creativity has always been a form of resistance, and these women wielded it with courage. They composed music when women were told to remain silent, painted self-portraits proudly when women like them were never represented on a canvas, and used cameras, stages, and microphones to tell truths that power tried to suppress.

Their work was not just about beauty:it was about survival, justice, and the radical act of self-expression. By blending tradition with innovation, they preserved cultural memory, and at the same time invented entirely new forms. They proved that art could dismantle stereotypes, carry the voice of the oppressed, and pave the way for others to follow. These women remind us that culture is not just inherited:it is created and protected, and has the power to change the world for future generations.

CHIQUINHA GONZAGA: THE PIANIST WHO BLENDED CULTURES AND BROKE BARRIERS

Francisca Edwiges Neves Gonzaga:known to generations as Chiquinha Gonzaga:was more than a composer. She was a cultural trailblazer, a freedom fighter, and a woman who defied every expectation placed on her in nineteenth-century Brazil. Her music didn't just entertain; it broke barriers.

Born in Rio de Janeiro in 1847, Chiquinha was the daughter of José Neves Gonzaga, a white aristocratic military officer, and Maria Rosa de Lima, a woman of African descent who had been born into slavery and later freed. Their relationship defied Brazil's rigid racial and social codes:and so would their daughter's life.

From a young age, Chiquinha was immersed in both classical European education and the vibrant, rhythmic traditions of Afro-Brazilian culture. At just eleven, she composed her first piece, *Canção dos Pastores*. But her father had other plans: At sixteen, she was married off to a naval officer. Her husband demanded she give up music. Her answer? "Sir, I do not understand life without harmony." She left him, and with that decision, she also lost custody of her children and was disowned by her family. In a society that judged and punished women for asserting independence, Chiquinha's choice was revolutionary.

She stepped into a world that was unforgiving to women:especially Black and mixed-race women:but Chiquinha forged a path all her own. Rejected by the elite, she found a home among Rio's artists and musicians. There, she composed, performed, and published music that blended European styles with Afro-Brazilian rhythms like the *lundu, maxixe,* and *choro.* These styles, once dismissed as vulgar, became the pulse of a new national identity:and Chiquinha was at the heart of it.

She was the first woman conductor in Brazil, the first female professional composer, and the first Brazilian woman to make a living as a musician. Her compositions:over three hundred pieces, including 77 works for the stage:spanned waltzes, tangos, operettas, and the iconic carnival anthem *"Ó Abre Alas,"* which is still sung during Brazilian *Carnaval* today.

But Chiquinha's influence didn't stop at music. She was an abolitionist who used her art and fame to support the end of slavery. She also co-founded the Brazilian Society of Theatrical Authors (SBAT) to defend artists' rights:making her a pioneer not just in sound, but in legal and labor protections for creatives.

Chiquinha lived to the age of eighty-seven, composing and performing until the very end. Today, she is honored as a founding mother of Brazilian popular music, and her birthday, October 17, is celebrated as the National Day of Brazilian Popular Music.

She was entirely ahead of her time, and her contributions to music and culture will never be forgotten.

TERESA CARREÑO: THE VALKYRIE *VENEZOLANA* OF THE PIANO

Teresa Carreño (1853–1917) was a Venezuelan pianist, composer, singer, and trailblazer whose talent electrified audiences across the globe.

Born in Caracas to a musical and politically active family, Teresa's brilliance emerged early. She began piano lessons at six under her father, Manuel Antonio Carreño, and within two years was performing in public. In 1862, after her family emigrated to New York, the eight-year-old prodigy made her dazzling debut at Irving Hall. A year later, she played for Abraham Lincoln at the White House:a sign of the international acclaim that awaited her.

By her teens, Carreño was touring Europe, studying under some of the most respected musicians of her day, including Georges Mathias, a pupil of Chopin, and Anton Rubinstein. Though Franz Liszt himself offered her lessons, she boldly declined. Carreño carved her own path, balancing the influence of the great European masters with her Venezuelan roots.

Her career spanned more than five decades and five continents. She toured relentlessly, performing in Europe, the Americas, Africa, and Australia. Critics and audiences alike marveled at her strength and elegance, her precision in octave passages, and her ability to command the stage with both dignity and fire. Sir Henry Wood, the British conductor, once wrote that she "looked like a queen among pianists:and played like a goddess."

Beyond performing, Carreño composed around eighty works, from virtuosic piano waltzes to chamber pieces and orchestral serenades. She infused her music with both European Romanticism and the rhythmic pulse of Venezuelan traditions. Her book *Possibilities of Tone Color by Artistic Use of Pedals*, published posthumously in 1919, remains a testament to her innovative approach to the piano.

Today, her spirit lives on in recordings, piano rolls, and the Teresa Carreño Cultural Complex in Caracas, one of Venezuela's most important concert halls.

Carreño broke through walls that were nearly impenetrable for women at the time. Music:even today:is dominated by men, especially at its highest levels of performance and composition. For a woman in the nineteenth century to tour the world's great stages, compose orchestral works, and publish books on piano technique was nothing short of revolutionary. She wasn't just participating in a male-dominated world:she was commanding it.

OMARA PORTUONDO: THE VOICE OF CUBA

Omara Portuondo has spent over seven decades serenading genera-tions of Cubans:and the world:with her soulful, jazz-inflected take on Cuban music. A pioneer of the *filin* movement and the only female star of the Buena Vista Social Club, Omara didn't just survive the twentieth century:she soundtracked it.

Born in Havana on October 29, 1930, Omara was raised in the culturally rich neighborhood of Cayo Hueso, where the air pulsed with music. Her mother, Esperanza Peláez, came from a wealthy white Spanish family, while her father, Bartolo Portuondo, was a Black baseball player who had played in the American Negro leagues. Their interracial marriage defied societal norms and was a source of scandal, but their home was filled with love, music, and resistance:a combination that would shape Omara's entire life.

As a teenager, Omara began her career as a dancer at the legendary Tropicana Club, Cuba's glamorous pre-revolutionary nightspot. But it wasn't long before she traded in dance steps for vocal lines. Singing with the band *Loquibambia* Swing and pianist Frank Emilio, she became a central figure in the *filin* movement:a Cuban style that mixed romantic American jazz ballads with Afro-Cuban rhythms. The public quickly dubbed her *La Novia del Filin*:the Girlfriend of Feeling.

In the 1950s, she and her sister Haydee co-founded *Cuarteto d'Aida*, an all-women vocal group that brought harmony, style, and sass to stages across Cuba and abroad. They sang backup for stars like Nat

King Cole and Benny Moré, toured internationally, and gained acclaim across the US, France, and Spain.

But history intervened. During a tour in Miami in 1962, the Cuban Missile Crisis erupted. Haydee and many other Cuban performers chose to stay in the US:Omara returned home. That decision wasn't just patriotic; it defined the rest of her life. At a time when many Cuban artists were fleeing the island, Omara became Cuba's voice abroad. Through the Cold War, revolutions, and decades of embargo, her voice continued to soar:from Havana to Helsinki, from Paris to Tokyo.

Her solo career blossomed, especially through her heartrending interpretations of *boleros*, *guarachas*, and Afro-Cuban jazz. She sang tributes to Che Guevara, Salvador Allende, and the Cuban Revolution, while also recording songs about love, heartbreak, and resistance. Her voice, often compared to Billie Holiday or Edith Piaf, could hold both grief and joy in a single phrase.

Then, in her late sixties, something extraordinary happened.

In 1996, Omara was invited to sing on *Buena Vista Social Club*, a Ry Cooder-produced album that brought together legendary, long-overlooked Cuban musicians. Omara became the group's only woman:and its beating heart. Her duet *"Silencio"* with Ibrahim Ferrer in Wim Wenders's documentary brought audiences to tears. For many viewers, Omara was the soul of the film, her eyes misty with memory as her voice soared.

The album was a global phenomenon. And just like that, Omara, at nearly seventy, became an international star. She toured the world, recorded Grammy-nominated albums, and even performed at Carnegie Hall. Her solo work:including *Flor de Amor* and *Gracias*:continued to spotlight her incredible vocal power and emotional depth.

She became the first Cuban woman appointed an International Ambassador for the Red Cross, sang on stages from the Royal Opera House in London to festivals in Asia, and collaborated with artists like Chucho Valdés and Maria Bethânia. Through it all, she remained deeply rooted in Havana, in her apartment overlooking the *Malecón*, never far from the music that raised her.

Omara is a living archive of Cuba's musical soul, a woman whose voice has carried the stories of generations.

SARA GÓMEZ: THE FILMMAKER WHO GAVE CUBA'S MARGINALIZED A VOICE

Sara Gómez was a visionary. A Black Cuban woman, a trained ethnographer, and a fierce cultural observer, she was the first female filmmaker of the Cuban Institute of Cinematographic Art and Industry (ICAIC), and the first Cuban woman to direct a feature film. In her short life, she transformed cinema into a tool for liberation:centering stories that had long been silenced.

Born in Havana in 1942 into a middle-class family, Gómez studied music and ethnography before entering the world of film. She came of age during the Cuban Revolution and saw its promise with clear eyes:hopeful, yet critical. Her camera became a portal into the everyday struggles of Cuba's Black, working-class, and female citizens. Her work explored themes still urgent today: racism, machismo, inequality, and the contradictions of revolutionary ideals.

Her early documentaries:*Guanabacoa: Chronicle of My Family* (1966), *La Otra Isla* (1968), and *Sobre Horas Extras y Trabajo Voluntario* (1973):blended oral history, archival footage, and vérité techniques. She captured everything from racial segregation to urban redevelopment and the gendered labor divide. Gómez didn't just observe:she participated. In *Mi Aporte* (1972), she joins a group of working women in a roundtable discussion about domestic expectations and workplace inequality, blurring the line between filmmaker and subject.

Her only feature film, *De Cierta Manera* (*One Way or Another*), was groundbreaking in both form and content. Blending documentary and fiction, it follows Yolanda, a light-skinned teacher, and Mario, a Black factory worker, as they navigate love, class tensions, and revolutionary ideals in a newly developed Havana neighborhood. The film interrogates machismo, privilege, and the limits of ideological transformation.

Tragically, Gómez died at just thirty-one due to a severe asthma attack, before completing the film. But *De Cierta Manera*, finished posthumously by her colleagues, remains a masterpiece:both a culmination of her artistic evolution and a call to action.

Sara Gómez told stories others couldn't or wouldn't. She humanized people left out of the national narrative and demanded that cinema reflect the complexities of real life. In doing so, she opened the door for a generation of Latina filmmakers ready to challenge systems and reshape representation.

Her life was brief:but her legacy is revolutionary.

JUNE BEER: THE AFRO-NICARAGUAN ARTIST WHO PAINTED HER PEOPLE INTO HISTORY

June Beer was a painter, poet, and pioneer:an Afro-Nicaraguan woman who made her Caribbean coast visible in a country that had long ignored it. Born in Bluefields, Nicaragua, on May 17, 1935, Beer was the first woman poet from the Atlantic Coast and one of the most radical artistic voices of her time. She was entirely self-taught, unafraid to disrupt both artistic and political norms, and deeply committed to telling the stories of her people in their own language, colors, and voices.

Raised in a community rich in Afro-Caribbean and Indigenous heritage, Beer embraced her Creole identity with pride. She wrote poetry in Creole English, Spanish, and occasionally in Miskito, capturing the linguistic complexity of Nicaragua's eastern coast. Through both words and paint, she chronicled the lives of Black women, workers, children, and communities often left out of national narratives.

At nineteen, she migrated to Los Angeles in search of work and became an artist's model. It was there, while posing for African American actress Ruby Dee, that she first expressed a desire to paint. Dee gifted her a set of art supplies:and Beer never looked back. Her first painting was a nude self-portrait, a bold and personal act of artistic self-claiming that would define her career.

Beer returned to Nicaragua, where her work stood apart from the abstract styles dominating the art scene. She rejected European techniques and themes in favor of Caribbean landscapes, Afro-Nicaraguan faces, and everyday life. She painted market women, mothers, and schoolgirls:not as exotic symbols, but as powerful, present, and real. Her feminism was unapologetic. Her racial politics were explicit. She was imprisoned twice by the Somoza dictatorship for her outspoken political views and later fled to Costa Rica, during the Sandinista Revolution.

Though she faced criticism and marginalization in her lifetime, Beer's impact was undeniable. Her paintings were eventually declared national patrimony, and her poems were recognized for their cultural and linguistic importance. She also wrote for *Sunrise*, a bilingual newspaper that gave voice to coastal communities often erased from national discourse.

June Beer died in 1986, at just fifty. But her legacy lives on in every stroke of color and every verse that centers Black Nicaraguan women as subjects, not symbols. She made history by refusing invisibility:and in doing so, created space for others to do the same.

PAZ ERRÁZURIZ: THE CHILEAN PHOTOGRAPHER WHO DARED TO LOOK

Paz Errázuriz didn't just take photographs:she bore witness. Born in Santiago, Chile, in 1944, she began her photography career in the 1970s as a self-taught artist during the height of the Pinochet dictatorship. While many used photography to document protest or violence, Errázuriz turned her lens toward those whom society:and the regime:preferred to forget: sex workers, trans women, psychiatric patients, boxers, the elderly, and the poor.

Errázuriz's work stands apart for its depth of intimacy and political metaphor. She didn't just "capture" her subjects; she built relationships with them. Her method was immersive: She lived in hospitals, spent weeks getting to know people, and often collaborated with women writers like Diamela Eltit and Claudia Donoso to publish photo essays that merged image and narrative. "I never photograph anyone straight away," she has said. "You have to be patient. You also have to be obsessed."

In *La Manzana de Adán* (1982–1990), she documented the daily lives of three trans women working in brothels in Talca and Santiago. The series, which showed the women with tenderness and respect, broke taboos and offered an unflinching look at gender, sexuality, and survival. In *El Infarto del Alma* (1994), she turned her camera toward psychiatric patients in Putaendo, revealing their romantic relationships and emotional lives:stories often erased by institutionalization.

Errázuriz co-founded the *Asociación de Fotógrafos Independientes* (AFI) in 1981, working independently from state media to protect artistic freedom during one of the darkest periods of Chilean history. Her work has since been shown internationally, including at the Venice Biennale and in the collections of MoMA, Tate Modern, and the Museo Reina Sofía. In 2017, she received Chile's National Prize for Fine Arts.

Her photographs are powerful because they carry both empathy and resistance. In a country under authoritarian rule, she learned to "speak in metaphor," creating images that revealed more than they stated, and humanizing lives that power tried to erase.

Even in her eighties, Paz Errázuriz is still being honored with major retrospectives. She continues to teach us that visibility is a radical act:and that the camera, in the right hands, can be a tool for revolution, reflection, and radical love.

RITA MORENO: THE TRAILBLAZING STAR WHO REFUSED TO BE BOXED IN

Rita Moreno is more than an icon:she is a force. With a career spanning over seventy years, Moreno shattered barriers in Hollywood and became the first Latina to achieve EGOT status, winning an Emmy, Grammy, Oscar, and Tony. But behind every accolade is a story of grit, grace, and groundbreaking perseverance.

Born Rosa Dolores Alverío in Humacao, Puerto Rico, in 1931, Moreno moved to New York City at age five with her mother, who worked as a seamstress. By eleven, Moreno was dubbing Spanish versions of American films; by thirteen, she was on Broadway. Soon after, she signed a contract with MGM and became "Rita Moreno":but the studio system had little imagination for Latina talent. She was often cast as the "exotic other," playing characters of various nonwhite ethnicities, always with an accent, always stereotyped.

In 1961, she landed her breakthrough role as Anita in *West Side Story*. Her fiery performance earned her an Academy Award, making her the first Latina to win an Oscar. But even with Hollywood's highest honor, the offers didn't change. Still pigeonholed into narrow roles, Moreno walked away from the industry, choosing instead to perform in summer theater and stage productions where her talent could breathe.

Her comeback in the 1970s was a master class in resilience. She starred in *The Electric Company*, which earned a Grammy for its soundtrack, and won a Tony for her performance in *The Ritz*. In 1977, she won back-to-back Emmys, completing her EGOT and cementing her legacy. Because of her commitment to her field, in 2019 Moreno was awarded a Peabody Career Achievement Award, establishing her as the first person of Latino/Latine descent to receive the honor.

But Moreno didn't stop there. From voicing Carmen Sandiego to starring in HBO's *Oz* and Netflix's *One Day at a Time*, she has remained a vital presence on screen. She even executive-produced and starred in the 2021 *West Side Story* remake, portraying a reimagined character, Valentina.

Along the way, Moreno has spoken candidly about the racism, sexism, and tokenism she endured in Hollywood. Her willingness to revisit the struggles behind the spotlight:through documentaries like *Just a Girl Who Decided to Go For It*:has made her a mentor to generations.

Today, Rita Moreno is not just a performer; she is a cultural institution, a *pionera* whose talent and advocacy continue to open doors for Latinas in entertainment. She didn't just survive Hollywood:she transformed it.

RENATA FLORES: THE QUEEN OF QUECHUA TRAP CREATING A CULTURAL REVOLUTION

Renata Flores is redefining what it means to be an Indigenous artist in the twenty-first century. Born in 2001 in Ayacucho, Peru, she has become one of the most powerful voices of her generation:literally:by fusing traditional Andean music with trap, hip hop, and pop, all while singing in Quechua, the Indigenous language of her ancestors. Her music is a cultural revolution wrapped in electronic beats.

Flores first captured global attention in 2015, when she uploaded a Quechua-language cover of Michael Jackson's "The Way You Make Me Feel" to YouTube. Set against the mountainous backdrop of the Pampa de la Quinua, the video went viral and sparked a national conversation about Quechua, a language often dismissed as outdated or rural. Her success marked a turning point:not just for Indigenous music, but for Indigenous identity in Peru and beyond.

Since then, she's used her platform to fight discrimination, elevate Andean culture, and make Quechua accessible to younger generations. "Music is the universal language," she says. "But Quechua is the language of my soul." Her lyrics, often co-written with her mother and manager Patricia Rivera, tackle issues like gender violence, racism, and historical erasure. Songs like *"Tijeras," "Mirando la Misma Luna,"* and *"Qam Hina"* are unapologetically political and deeply poetic.

Her first album, *Isqun* (which means "nine" in Quechua), paid tribute to powerful women in Peruvian history. Her second album, *Traficante*, reflects a more personal journey:one rooted in her hometown of Huamanga and shaped by her family's resilience.

Renata's performances are equal parts music and movement. Her choreography, visuals, and wardrobe are steeped in Andean aesthetics, yet undeniably futuristic. In 2025, she'll represent Peru at the Viña del Mar Festival with *"Kuti Tika"* ("Bloom Again"), a high-energy anthem that celebrates growth and renewal.

International media has taken notice. She's been profiled by *The New York Times*, BBC, *Hola!*, VICE, and *Forbes Perú*, which named her one of the country's most powerful and influential women. Still, Flores remains grounded in her mission: to preserve Quechua and empower Indigenous youth.

"I don't want to make songs about nothing," she says. "I want them to reach people." And they do:because Renata Flores isn't just singing in Quechua; she's singing with heart, with purpose, and with a mission to make Indigenous voices heard. In an industry that's already hard enough to break into as a woman, Renata is proving that you don't have to leave your culture behind to succeed. By blending tradition with modernity, she's telling stories that resonate across generations:and that, in itself, is revolutionary.

FRIDA KAHLO:THE UNCOMPROMISING ARTIST WHO INSPIRED WOMEN EVERYWHERE

As the famous saying by Laurel Thatcher Ulrich goes, "Well-behaved women seldom make history." Frida is a shining beacon of what Latinas can achieve when they lean into who they are at their core and proceed to take on the world in a fearless fashion. The Mexican painter was born July 6, 1907, in Coyoacán and quickly became known for her unique style that was shaped by themes of identity, the human body, and death.

Frida lived a complex life:dealing with a host of health problems and an often fraught relationship with her husband and muralist Diego Rivera. The union of her *mestiza* mother and her father, a German of Hungarian descent, made her consistently explore the juxtaposition of her indigenous and European backgrounds. This is why many of her works feature bright colors with elements of Realism, Surrealism, and Symbolism.

For her, her art was an extension of her feelings and a vehicle for self-expression, with each painting being an intimate view into her world. Her pain, loss, and passion were etched into every self-portrait, reflecting a reality she could not escape. Throughout her career, she produced approximately 200 paintings, sketches, and drawings.

While many branded her a Surrealist, she rejected the title, noting that there was nothing surreal about her artwork because she was painting the reality of her life. Despite her prolific work, she wouldn't sell much of it during her lifetime. This is a stark contrast to the reality of her artwork today.

In 2006, her self-portrait *Roots* sold at auction for $5.62 million in New York City, setting a record for the most expensive Latin American work ever bought at an auction house. That sale solidified her as one of the highest-selling female painters. Later, in 2025, her self-portrait *El sueño* (*La cama*) sold at auction for $54.7 million. It's no surprise that her work has resonated with people years after her passing. Her raw honesty, courage, and conviction are universal themes that will resonate with generations to come.

AMERICA FERRERA: THE ACTRESS TURNED ACTIVIST

Representation matters. Seeing yourself and your culture's stories reflected in the media, on TV, and in film is important. Like many within creative fields, America knew at a young age that her path, whatever it may be, would involve acting. In the years since, she has carved out a career that has established her as an Oscar-worthy talent.

The actress was born on April 18, 1984, in Los Angeles, California to Honduran immigrant parents who came to the United States in the 1970s. The youngest of six children, America was bitten by the acting bug at the age of seven, when she participated in her elementary school's production of *Hamlet*. She continued pursuing this passion throughout her school career and landed her first film role in the 2002 Disney Channel movie "Gotta Kick It Up!" That same year, she appeared in the acclaimed coming-of-age film *Real Women Have Curves*.

While studying international relations and theater at the University of Southern California, she landed roles in *How the Garcia Girls Spent Their Summer* and *The Sisterhood of the Traveling Pants*. But it was her role on *Ugly Betty* that solidified her stardom, earning her a Golden Globe Award and a Screen Actors Guild Award.

America also won an Emmy Award for her role on the show, making her the first Latina to win Outstanding Lead Actress in a Comedy Series. As her star rose, so did the possibilities for what she could carve out for herself. The actress went on to become both a director and a producer in her own right, working on projects like Netflix's *Gentefied* and NBC's *Superstore*.

America's most significant role was as Gloria in Greta Gerwig's 2023 film *Barbie*, where she delivered a breathtaking monologue about the difficulties women experience trying to live up to society's demanding standards for who they should be. Greta was said to have written the role with the actress in mind, with the monologue serving as an extension of all the work that America has done off-screen.

When she's not acting, producing, or directing, she is staunchly advocating for women's rights, gender equality within the entertainment industry, immigration reform, racial justice, and environmental conservation. In 2019, she gave a moving TED Talk, "My Identity Is a Superpower:Not an Obstacle," where she discussed how embracing her background is a strength.

She has attached herself to organizations such as Families Belong Together and the Time's Up Legal Defense Fund, and also joined the #MeToo and She Se Puede, campaigns. In 2024, she was named a Global Goodwill Ambassador for the International Organization for Migration.

"Feet, what do I need them for if I have wings to fly?"

FRIDA KAHLO, MEXICAN PAINTER KNOWN
FOR EXPLORING THEMES OF IDENTITY, THE
BODY, AND DEATH, WHILE INCORPORATING
MEXICAN CULTURE AND INDIGENOUS
SYMBOLISM

SIX

MUJERES INDOMABLES

ATHLETES AND TRAILBLAZERS IN SPORTS

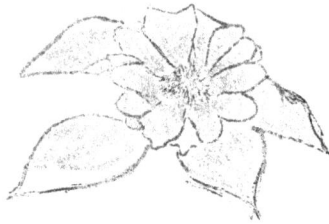

It's easy to remember the first time we see a female athlete dominate on a field or court. They captivate with their grace, resolve, courage, and boldness. They lead by example and ensure that they are setting the standard for what it means to be an athlete. These women are running, weaving, sweating, and crying, all in the name of a higher calling that they cannot live without.

They are the embodiment of excellence, and without realizing it, they inspire little girls everywhere to dream bigger than they thought possible. However, reducing these elite athletes to just women who play a sport would be a disservice to all those who came before and will come after. That passion you see on the field? Well, they carry that off the field as well.

They will fight for their rights as fiercely as they fight for that extra goal or point. They will work tirelessly to ensure that, when the time comes, future athletes will benefit from the things they have always deserved. These women will level the playing field and guarantee that no future woman has to start with zero on the scoreboard. The women in this chapter aren't just untamable athletes; they are Latinas who are the manifestation of a fire that will never die.

MARTA VIEIRA DA SILVA: THE RECORD BREAKER

Rising to the top doesn't always require a lot of fancy footwork. Oftentimes, all you need is a passion, preparation, and drive. Greatest of all time isn't a title that is given lightly. For Marta, being considered the greatest female *fútbol* player of all time was decades in the making.

Marta was born in Dois Riachos, Brazil, on February 19, 1986, and had it been left up to her male peers, she might have never touched a soccer ball in her life. The Brazilian athlete emerged in a time not long after the ban on women playing the sport:enacted in 1941 because it was deemed contrary to their nature:was lifted in 1979. Despite the ability of women to play, the resistance she encountered saw her get creative and practice kicking around with improvised balls.

When she was fourteen, she was discovered by Vasco da Gama while playing *fútbol* on a local boys' junior team, and subsequently joined a women's team out of Rio de Janeiro. In 2004, she relocated to Sweden to play for the Umeå IK and gained widespread popularity and renown. From 2005 to 2008, she helped the team achieve four consecutive Swedish soccer championships. Marta ultimately scored 111 goals during the 103 league games she played over the five years she was there.

In 2009, she relocated to the United States and played for several teams, including the Los Angeles Sol, FC Gold Pride of Santa Clara, the New York Flash, and the Orlando Pride. While Marta always gave it her all on the soccer pitch, for her there was no greater love than playing for the Brazilian national team:something that cemented her place in sports history.

In 2002, she made her international debut as a member of the team, but it wasn't until 2003 that she landed on the senior national team and scored her first three goals for her country at the FIFA Women's World Cup. Marta went on to score seventeen World Cup goals, a record that marked her as the all-time leading scorer in both women's and men's World Cup competitions.

At the 2020 Tokyo Games, she became the first *fútbol* player to score a goal in five consecutive Olympics. Alongside her teammates, she helped Brazil attain three silver medals, officially stepping down from playing for the team in 2024.

SYLVIA + CLAUDIA POLL AHRENS: THE SISTERS WHO LED THEIR COUNTRY TO GLORY

Competing in the Olympics is no easy feat. The journey and road that lead to the Olympics is often much harder. The first modern games were hosted in Greece in 1896, and since then, more and more countries have gradually joined in participating. While they came from one of the smaller participating countries, sisters Sylvia and Claudia proved that you don't need to come from a powerhouse country to win big.

Born on September 24, 1970, in Managua, Nicaragua, Sylvia is the oldest of the two sisters and the first athlete to win a medal for Costa

Rica at the Olympics. While competing in the 1988 Seoul Olympics, Sylvia earned the silver medal for the 200-meter freestyle swimming category. Her medal also marked the first medal achieved by a Central American athlete since the beginning of the modern games.

She shared in an interview, "The first thing I remember is that I saw the results and I couldn't believe it. It's a strange feeling because it's something you've worked so hard for, even enduring the death of my father, that at that moment you can't digest everything at the same speed."

While Sylva competed in the Barcelona games as well, she did not manage to medal in the swimming disciplines she competed in. Her younger sister, Claudia, born on December 21, 1972, also went on to compete in the Olympics. In the 1996 Atlanta Olympic Games, Claudia won Costa Rica's first gold medal for the 200-meter freestyle swimming race.

Much like her older sister, she went on to compete in an additional Olympics and won two bronze medals during the 2000 Sydney Olympics. Outside of the games, both sisters have competed and placed high at world competitions for their respective disciplines on behalf of Costa Rica.

MARILEIDY PAULINO: THE SPRINTING QUEEN OF THE DOMINICAN REPUBLIC

Running is one of the earliest things we learn to do as children. Whether you are running in a race or playing tag, there is a freedom in running that little else can compare to. And, if you're disciplined enough, like Marileidy, running can win you a gold medal.

Born October 25, 1996, in Nizao, the decorated sprinter is one of six children, and didn't grow up with the strict sporting background many would think was indicative of future Olympic athletes. Because she came from a larger family, she grew up in an environment where each person in the house had to contribute to the overall success of the family.

She once told sports writer Yancel Pujols that she "used to clean houses in exchange for food [...] because things were difficult at home." This focus on survival meant that Marileidy grew up only playing pick-up sports and participating in the odd school team as a child. But when she was in high school, her innate talent and athleticism were palpably undeniable.

She was recruited to the Dominican Republic's Athletics Federation. Once there, she began practicing in track and field barefoot. Marileidy has since trained for the 400-meter sprint, the 4x100-meter relay, and the 4x400-meter mixed relay. The Dominican sprinter has competed at the World Athletics Championships, Ibero-American Championships, and World Relay Championships. She has also served as a corporal in the Dominican Air Force, which made her eligible to participate in the World Military Games.

However, it wasn't until the 2020 Tokyo Olympics that Marileidy took the international stage by storm, winning the silver medal in the 400-meter race. She continued to solidify her claim as a sprinter with a bright future when she ran her leg of the mixed 4x400-meter mixed relay in 48.7 seconds at the World Athletics Championships in both 2021 and 2022.

By 2023, the *Dominicana* was ranked No. 1 in the world for her discipline. Then, at the 2024 Paris Olympics, she made history as the first woman from the Dominican Republic to earn a gold medal in any sport. She ran a remarkable 48.17-second 400-meter race, bringing her country's medal count up to three.

CHOLITAS LUCHADORAS: THE INDIGENOUS WRESTLERS FIGHTING FOR EQUALITY

Regardless of their country of origin or cultural heritage, every athlete is proud to represent their roots. When part of your lived experience has been marred by oppression, injustice, and violence, honoring your roots becomes a battle cry. For Bolivia's *Cholitas Luchadoras,* owning their Indigenous roots with unapologetic pride, dignity, and honor has been the fire that powers their sense of purpose and drive.

When many think about wrestlers, they don't typically think of small-statured Indigenous women in skirts, petticoats, hand-woven pieces, and bowler hats. Most will think of the *luchadores* of Mexico or the spandex-clad wrestlers of the United States. Thankfully, the world has the gift that is Bolivia's *Cholitas,* who, with every wrestling match, flip the script on what it means to be unrepentantly you, but also what Latinas and Indigenous women are capable of.

Like many Indigenous people in Latin America, *Cholitas* have faced their fair share of ostracization for decades. For centuries, these women were seen as second-class citizens. These women, typically of Quechuan and Aymaran ethnic descent, were often relegated to cleaning homes and barred from higher education. But when they step into the ring, they reclaim centuries of stolen power through the force of their strength and prominent sense of identity.

Much like typical wrestling matches, each wrestling match has its *técnicos* (heroes) and its *rudos* (villains). Audiences are in for a feast of fun, action, drama, music, and even some of the *Cholitas* fighting men. The women are often the fan favorites in those fights as well. But this show of strength hasn't just stayed within the ring.

Under former President Juan Evo Morales Ayma, typically referred to as Evo Morales, the Indigenous communities of Bolivia were able to flourish. As the country's first Indigenous president, his presence opened the path for more Indigenous people to pursue opportunities outside of what society had consigned them to. What does this mean for *Cholitas?* Many of them were able to run for government positions.

Wrestling isn't the only sport you'll catch *Cholitas* in:they've also taken up mountain climbing and *fútbol.* All in their beautiful, traditional attire.

IMILLASKATE: THE *POLLERA*-WEARING SKATERS BUILDING COMMUNITY

Skateboarding is a sport that has historical and cultural ties to the surfboarding and land surfing practices of the Indigenous Native Hawaiians. As its natural progression, skateboarding offers a freedom to riders that not much else does. For ImillaSkate, it's a chance for them to tap into their sense of sisterhood, identity, and fierce internal power.

Much like the *Cholita Luchadoras, las chicas de* ImillaSkate stand out for two reasons: their nod to their indigenous roots and the fact that they are dominating a sport thought to be for *los chicos.* The group, founded in 2019 by two friends, got together in an effort to create a space where they felt included. *Imilla*, which means "young girl" in Aymara and Quechua, is a nod to Bolivia's vibrant and often ignored indigenous roots. The group has grown to include more women since then.

Unlike the *polleras* worn by the *Cholita Luchadoras* in La Paz, Imilla-Skate's skateboarding outfit is a bit more flowy, loose, and shorter. But the clothes are equally as bright and showstopping. The Cochabamba-born women have noted that the vibrant colors of their *polleras* help them to feel more powerful.

So, why skateboarding? Because of the inclusive nature of the sport. María Belén Fajardo Fernández, one of the members of the group, has stated that the sport "doesn't discriminate" against age, gender, or what you look like. It's a sport that's focused on you being happy and loving what you are doing. Many of the women have noted how, after joining ImillaSkate, the empowering feeling they get when they skate has carried over into other areas of their lives.

But at the end of the day, the collective sisterhood and desire to protect an essential aspect of their culture are the glue that keeps it all together. From the intentionality of their long braids to their *pollera* skirts and the hats they wear:it is all for the love of their community (and the game).

MARÍA LORENA RAMÍREZ HERNÁNDEZ: THE ONE WHO NEVER STOPPED RUNNING

To run is to have a tremendous amount of endurance, perseverance, and steadfast grit. When it comes to long-distance running, it's a whole other ballgame. As a runner, María Lorena's determination captured the hearts and attention of women everywhere, proving that women could and can truly do anything they set their minds to, regardless of what they are wearing.

María Lorena, born January 1, 1995, comes from a family of runners and follows in the footsteps of her brother, father, and grandfather. But for her, it went beyond her familial ties; she sees running as a way to connect with her community and with nature, and as a way of life. For her, running was an intrinsic and integral part of who she was, which influenced why she has been running all of her life.

The standout moment that thrust her onto the international stage came when she ran 50 kilometers (roughly 31.07 miles) in the Cerro Rojo UltraTrail in 2017, wearing the traditional clothing of her community and relying only on huaraches for footwear.

Her decision to use huaraches was also highly celebrated as it highlighted her indigenous Rarámuri roots. María Lorena is seen as a beacon for indigenous women and Latinas everywhere to remember that their sense of identity is their superpower. It is something that should be shown off to the world proudly, loudly, and without faltering.

In January 2025, she competed in one of the most grueling long-distance races ever when she participated in the Hong Kong 100 Ultra Marathon. The competition hosted about two thousand international runners. Despite some setbacks, María Lorena placed 328th in the women's category and ran a time of twenty-six hours, two minutes, and twelve seconds. With each race that she competes in, she solidifies a legacy that will uplift not only the Rarámuri community, but female runners everywhere.

"I have gotten into a lot of trouble in my life for being brutally honest. Sometimes I put both my feet in my mouth. But like Elton John, I'm still standing."

CRISTINA SARALEGUI, CUBAN-BORN
JOURNALIST WHO WAS THE FIRST AND ONLY
LATINA TO HAVE A SUCCESSFUL RADIO
SHOW, A WIDELY CIRCULATED
MAGAZINE, AND A TALK SHOW, ALL AT THE
SAME TIME.

SEVEN
REBELS AND REVOLUTIONARIES
FIGHTERS FOR FREEDOM

History often remembers the generals, presidents, and statesmen who shaped nations. But behind every battle for independence, every movement for justice, and every defense of land, women were fighting too. They were spies and soldiers, educators and organizers, pilots and poets. They picked up rifles, stitched coded messages into clothing, and led guerrilla armies when men were gone. Some gave their lives on the battlefield; others rebuilt entire nations from ruins.

For centuries, their names were buried, their contributions dismissed as footnotes. Yet without them, the stories of freedom in Latin America would be incomplete. These women redefined what resis-

tance looked like. They fought colonial empires, challenged dictator-
ships, and protected ancestral lands from destruction. They proved
that courage is not limited by gender:and that the price of freedom is
often borne by those least recognized.

They were not the supporting cast of revolutions. They were the
revolution.

JUANA AZURDUY DE PADILLA: THE FORGOTTEN GENERAL OF SOUTH AMERICAN INDEPENDENCE

Juana Azurduy was a freedom fighter, revolutionary leader, and military strategist whose name should stand beside the great liberators of
Latin America:but for nearly two centuries, she was largely forgotten.
Born in 1780 in Chuquisaca (modern-day Sucre, Bolivia), she was a
mestiza woman who grew up between two worlds: her Spanish father
and Indigenous mother, and the deep cultural ties she maintained to
both.

After the death of her parents, Azurduy was sent to a convent, where
she famously idolized Joan of Arc and was expelled at seventeen for
her rebellious nature. In 1805, she married fellow revolutionary
Manuel Ascencio Padilla. Their bond was rare for the time:partners
in love and in battle. Together, they fought for Bolivia's independence from Spanish rule, commanding thousands of troops, forming
guerrilla armies, and recruiting Indigenous fighters and women
warriors known as the *Amazonas*.

Between 1811 and 1817, Juana Azurduy fought in over twenty
battles. Dressed in male cavalry uniform, she led a legendary charge
to capture the silver-rich Cerro Rico in Potosí and was later honored
by General Manuel Belgrano, who gifted her his sword and promoted
her to Lieutenant Colonel. She even returned to the battlefield just
hours after giving birth.

But her victories came at an unbearable cost. Her children died of disease and malnutrition in the harsh conditions of military camps:rumor has it that some of her children were captured and killed by the Spanish military. In 1816, her husband was killed trying to rescue her during the Battle of La Laguna, and his severed head was displayed by Spanish forces as a warning. Despite her injuries and grief, Juana returned to the battlefield:this time in mourning, dressed in black.

After independence was won, she returned to a life of poverty, erased from the nation she had helped liberate. Her pension was revoked, her contributions ignored. She died in 1862, buried in a communal grave, far from her hometown.

Only in recent years has Azurduy been recognized for her legacy. In 2009, Argentina posthumously promoted her to the rank of general. In 2015, a fifty-two-foot statue of her replaced one of Christopher Columbus in Buenos Aires. And yet:how many people still know her name?

Juana Azurduy gave everything: her children, her husband, her homeland, her body. And for decades, she got nothing in return. Her story reminds us that not all heroes are remembered:but they should be.

POLICARPA SALAVARRIETA: THE SPY WHO STITCHED A REVOLUTION

Policarpa Salavarrieta:better known as *La Pola*:seized every thread of opportunity to help unravel Spanish colonial rule in New Granada, the region that would become Colombia. Seamstress by trade, revolutionary by calling, and spy by necessity, she risked everything for a dream of independence. She paid the ultimate price, but not before establishing herself as one of the fiercest heroines in Latin American history.

Born in 1795 in Guaduas, Policarpa grew up amid growing political unrest. Her family, once considered respectable, was decimated by a smallpox epidemic, leaving her an orphan by age seven. She and her siblings returned to Guaduas under the care of their older sister and godmother. There, surrounded by patriots and ex-soldiers, she absorbed the spirit of resistance from a young age.

Her political activities intensified when she moved to Bogotá with her brother Bibiano. Living in the home of Andrea Ricaurte de Lozano:a hub for revolutionary planning:*La Pola* leveraged her skills as a seamstress to infiltrate the homes of Spanish officers. Underestimated due to her youth and gender, she listened, gathered intelligence, passed along messages, and helped recruit others to the cause. Her lover and fellow rebel, Alejo Sabaraín, often worked alongside her.

La Pola's cover was blown in 1817 after captured revolutionaries were found carrying incriminating documents linked to her. She destroyed everything she could before her arrest to protect her comrades. Despite being imprisoned and sentenced to death by firing squad, she refused to beg for mercy. On November 14, 1817, moments before her execution, she famously declared: "Although I am a woman and young, I have more than enough courage to suffer this death and a thousand more. Do not forget my example."

Policarpa's words echoed long after the gunfire ceased. Colombia gained independence in 1823, but her sacrifice had already fueled the fire for freedom. Today, she is honored as a national heroine:her image printed on currency, statues erected in her memory, and November 14 celebrated as the Day of the Colombian Woman.

In a revolution dominated by male figures, *La Pola* proved that courage has no gender. She didn't just sew garments:she helped stitch together a vision of liberation. And in doing so, she became a symbol of power, pride, and defiance for generations of Colombian women to come.

HERMELINDA URVINA: THE LATINA WHO TOUCHED THE SKY

Hermelinda Urvina Mayorga was a trailblazer in aviation and a pioneer for women across Latin America. Born on September 26, 1905, in Ambato, Ecuador, to José Bellisario Urbina and Felicidad Mayorga, she would become the first woman from South America to earn a pilot's license, breaking gender barriers at a time when few women had access to the skies.

At age twenty-one, Urvina married Rosendo Briones in 1926, and the couple moved to New York City, where they lived for nearly two decades. It was there that Hermelinda's fascination with flight became a career. In 1932, she earned her pilot's license from the Safair Flying School in Long Island, becoming a licensed aviator under the US Aeronautics Authority. That same year, she made history as the first South American woman to be officially recognized as a pilot.

Hermelinda didn't just fly:she soared. She was one of the founding members of the Ninety-Nines, a women's aviation organization in the United States. Through this group, she became close with other aviation legends, such as Amelia Earhart and Charles Lindbergh. Urvina participated in publicized flights, including a remarkable journey between New York and Washington, DC, which drew significant media attention and solidified her as a public figure in aviation circles.

She continued to fly throughout the 1930s, and even completed long-distance flights under harsh weather conditions, such as a challenging journey from New York to Montreal during which many other pilots were forced to abandon the route. In 1937, she was also awarded a Mexican pilot's license, allowing her to link air routes across the US, Mexico, and Canada. She later purchased a yellow airplane she named "Ecuador," enabling her to travel independently and represent her country in the skies.

In 1945, she returned to Ecuador and worked in the family business. Though she retired from flying, her spirit of adventure remained. In her later years, Hermelinda moved to Toronto to be closer to her daughter, Rosario, where she took up boating and snowmobiling:well into her nineties. She passed away on September 20, 2008, at age 103.

In 2000, the Ecuadorian press honored her as one of the "10 most influential women of the millennium." Hermelinda Urvina's legacy continues to inspire generations of women in Latin America and beyond.

YUTURI WARMI: AMAZON DEFENDERS ROOTED IN TRADITION AND RESISTANCE

In the heart of Ecuador's Amazon, along the Jatunyacu River in Napo province, a powerful group of Indigenous women has risen to defend their ancestral land from the threats of gold mining and environmental degradation. Known as *Yuturi Warmi:*"Bullet Ant Women" in Kichwa:they are the first all-women Indigenous guard in the region. Founded in 2020 by fourteen women from the Serena community, the group has since expanded to include nearly all the women of the area, ranging in age from twenty-three to eighty-five. Their name references the fierce yuturi ant, known for defending its territory with strength and unity.

More than environmentalists, these women are cultural guardians, blending ancestral spirituality with modern resistance. Their days begin with *Guayusa Upina*, a traditional dawn ceremony of tea and prayer, led by elder Corina Andy. They patrol thousands of acres of forest and riverbanks with drones and camera traps, looking for signs of illegal mining, and they meticulously document environmental damage to build legal and public cases for protection. Their territory remains one of the last clean stretches of river in a region increasingly scarred by contamination.

Yuturi Warmi's leadership has extended beyond the forest. The group has filed legal actions, coordinated with other Indigenous federations, and testified at national and international forums. In 2022, they played a key role in exposing unlicensed gold extraction in nearby Yutzupino, resulting in the confiscation of 107 excavators and a court order for environmental reparation. Yet enforcement remains weak, and their vigilance continues.

The group also provides alternatives to mining through economic and cultural initiatives:teaching artisanal crafts, promoting sustainable agriculture, and envisioning eco-tourism projects. Many members say the group has transformed their personal lives, giving them purpose, voice, and protection from gender-based violence. "In this community, we don't have drugs or crime:and we won't allow it," says co-leader Elsa Cerda.

Despite facing threats and political neglect, Yuturi Warmi remains unwavering. They are not only resisting extractivism:they are actively building a post-extractive future rooted in reciprocity, community, and care for the Earth. Their model of Indigenous women's leadership is reshaping what environmental defense looks like in the twenty-first century.

In the words of one member, "Real progress will not come from outside. It will come from us."

LAS RESIDENTAS: THE WOMEN WHO REBUILT PARAGUAY FROM ASHES

The War of the Triple Alliance (1864–1870) left Paraguay devastated. The country faced annihilation at the hands of Brazil, Argentina, and Uruguay:an alliance backed by British financial interests. In what remains one of the most brutal and disproportionate conflicts in Latin American history, Paraguay lost as much as 90% of its male population. But from this unimaginable tragedy arose a force of strength, resilience, and national rebirth: *Las Residentas.*

"*Residenta*" was not originally a formal title:it was a bureaucratic adaptation, likely born when women filling out relocation documents were labeled as female residents: *residentas*. But the name stuck, and it came to signify something far greater.

These were the women who kept Paraguay alive.

As the front lines pushed north and cities like Ñeembucú and Misiones were evacuated, women:often with young children in tow:traveled harsh roads to unfamiliar towns. There, they labored in fields under military discipline, growing crops, spinning cotton, and feeding a country at war. Others followed their husbands, fathers, and sons to the battlefield, supporting the logistics of an army in collapse. When no men were left to fight, some picked up rifles themselves.

They endured hunger, cold, and brutal violence. They buried the dead. They resisted with whatever they had:knives, stones, even glass. In towns like Piribebuy, women stood armed against enemy assaults. And after the last shot was fired at Cerro Corá, it was *Las Residentas* who returned to rebuild what remained.

There are few records of their names, but those we know deserve to be remembered.

Francisca Cabrera, a mother of four, armed her children and vowed to die fighting rather than surrender.

María Isabel Martínez de Caballero buried her husband after witnessing his execution, then returned home alone.

Juana Pabla Torres lost her parents defending her village and survived alongside her aunt.

Felicia Bado, María del Pilar Rojas de Velazco, and De los Ángeles Méndez are among others who walked these same roads.

These women:of all classes, ages, and backgrounds:repurposed grief into action. They not only sustained a country during its darkest hour; they also laid the foundations for its rebirth. They preserved the Guaraní language, rebuilt the economy, and passed down the soul of a nation.

SALOME UREÑA DE HENRIQUEZ: THE MOTHER OF DOMINICAN LETTERS

Salomé Ureña de Henríquez (1850–1897) is remembered as one of the Dominican Republic's most revered poets:and as a pioneering feminist educator whose life and legacy continue to shape the nation's cultural identity. Known for her passionate patriotism and devotion to education, Salomé's voice rang with both lyric tenderness and powerful political conviction.

Born in Santo Domingo to Nicolás Ureña de Mendoza, a respected writer and intellectual, and Gregoria Díaz de León, Salomé grew up in a household where books and ideas were daily bread. Her father tutored her personally, immersing her in classical Spanish literature and inspiring the early development of her literary voice. By age fifteen she was writing poetry, and at seventeen she published her first verses under the pseudonym Herminia:a strategic choice for a young woman navigating the male-dominated literary world of the nineteenth century.

Ureña's poetry celebrated the natural beauty of the island, the love of family, and the struggle for Dominican sovereignty. She infused her work with deep national pride, and poems like *"A la Patria"* and *"Ruinas"* have become enduring symbols of Dominican identity. Her tone, often described as *"viril y lleno de grandeza"* ("virile and full of grandeur"), defied the gender norms of her era and earned her both

admiration and criticism. Even Dominican president Joaquín Balaguer would later write of her *"acento poderosamente varonil"* ("pow-
erfully masculine accent"), reflecting how her bold style challenged
expectations of feminine writing.

But Salomé's impact extended far beyond the page. In 1881, she
founded the *Instituto de Señoritas*, the first institution of higher
learning for women in the Dominican Republic. With support from
her husband, Francisco Henríquez y Carvajal:who would later
become president of the country:Salomé trained a new generation of
women as teachers and leaders. The first six women ever to earn
teaching degrees in the DR were graduates of her school.

Her life was cut short at forty-seven, but Salomé Ureña's legacy is
profound. She was honored with a public funeral and remembered as
"madre, siempre madre":not only to her four children (including
noted intellectual Pedro Henríquez Ureña), but to the Dominican
nation. A statue of her stands today in Santo Domingo's Colonial
Zone, a tribute to a woman who proved that poetry and pedagogy
could both be revolutionary acts.

VICTORIA OCAMPO: THE PUBLISHER WHO BRIDGED CONTINENTS

Victoria Ocampo (1890–1979) was one of Argentina's most influential cultural figures of the twentieth century. A writer, editor, transla-
tor, and tireless promoter of international dialogue, she carved out a
place in a literary landscape dominated by men, proving that women
could not only participate in, but also lead, cultural movements.

Born in Buenos Aires into a wealthy family, Ocampo received an
education typical of elite women at the time:focused on languages,
music, and etiquette:but she defied expectations by dedicating her
life to letters. She published nearly twenty books of essays, collected
in her ten-volume *Testimonios*, where she combined political reflec-

tion, literary criticism, and autobiography. Her writing revealed both her personal struggles and her vision for Argentina's role in global culture.

Ocampo's greatest legacy was *Sur*, the magazine she founded in 1931, along with its publishing house two years later. For almost half a century, *Sur* was a hub for intellectual exchange between Latin America, North America, and Europe. It introduced Spanish-speaking audiences to global voices such as Virginia Woolf, Albert Camus, Jean-Paul Sartre, and William Faulkner:many of them translated by Ocampo herself. At the same time, she provided a platform for emerging Argentine writers, most famously Jorge Luis Borges, who published some of his best work in its pages.

Through *Sur*, Ocampo positioned Argentina as a cultural bridge during a period of intense political and intellectual upheaval. Yet she was not without controversy. Critics accused her of elitism, of relying too heavily on her wealth and class privilege, and of prioritizing European high culture over local traditions. She was often juxtaposed with Eva Perón: Ocampo representing aristocratic feminism, Evita embodying working-class populism. Their differences highlighted the tensions within Argentine society about class, gender, and power.

Beyond her literary endeavors, Ocampo was also a vocal advocate for women's rights. She co-founded the Argentine Women's Union, fought for women's access to education and political participation, and became the first woman admitted to the Argentine Academy of Letters in 1975. Her presence in such spaces challenged entrenched patriarchal norms, even as her feminism reflected the contradictions of her class.

When Ocampo died in 1979, she left behind an extraordinary cultural legacy. Admired and criticized in equal measure, she remains a symbol of intellectual independence and of the power of women to shape cultural history on their own terms. Through her writing, publishing, and advocacy, Victoria Ocampo opened doors for future generations of Latin American women to enter the world of ideas not as guests, but as leaders.

"You've got to believe. Never be afraid to dream."

GLORIA ESTEFAN, CUBAN-AMERICAN ARTIST,
AUTHOR, AND BUSINESSWOMAN WHO HAS
SOLD MORE THAN 100 MILLION ALBUMS
WORLDWIDE

EIGHT

HIDDEN FIGURES

GROUNDBREAKERS AND
TRAILBLAZERS IN UNEXPECTED PLACES

Women have been making moves for as long as anyone can remember. While some women received more recognition than others, the advances and contributions made by all women have lasting ramifications that will echo throughout time, space, and history. Women have invented life-changing gadgets, solved what many thought was an unsolvable problem, and showed up dressed in grit.

If a groundbreaker can't find a shovel to make room for something she knows is needed, she'll use her hands and break it open herself.

When a woman, especially a Latina, sets her mind to something, there is nothing she won't accomplish. She won't just manifest it; she will turn the wheels that make everything move and bend it to her will. She will help others rise with her because she understands that when one of us wins, we all do.

The women in this chapter may not have set out to bulldoze the barriers set before them, but their actions made it possible for others to follow in their footsteps.

CLARA GONZÁLEZ DE BEHRINGER: THE *PROFESORA* WHO KNEW CHILDREN DESERVED MORE

Clara was born in Remedios in the Republic of Panamá on September 11, 1898, to a Spanish father and a *mestiza* mother. However, when she was two years old, she and her family briefly relocated to Costa Rica after her father allegedly refused to supply weapons to a political party in Panamá.

The family eventually relocated to Panamá, and some time later, her mother, Basilia Carillo Sánchez, left the family. Clara would go on to be raised by her father, alongside her brother. Due to her father's nomadic work lifestyle, she and her brother grew up in poverty. Following the abandonment by her mother, it is said that Clara experienced a sexual assault at the age of seven at the hands of a family friend.

Notwithstanding, the experiences she had growing up were the foundation for what would become her life's work. Clara always showed a knack for learning, something her father always encouraged and nurtured in her.

She eventually attended school on a scholarship that her father was able to get for her at a religious all-girls school located in Panama City run by French nuns. Her ultimate goal was to become a lawyer and practice law in Panamá; unfortunately, this wasn't a dream she could pursue until later in life.

Despite the societal norms of the time, Clara refused to allow her future to be dictated. She later attended the Escuela Normal de Institutoras, where she earned a teaching degree, as that was the only profession available to women at the time. Regardless of what life and society allowed her to do, she remained a staunch advocate for the human rights of women and children.

While working as a teacher, she enrolled in the *Escuela de Derecho en el Instituto Nacional*. When she graduated, she became the first *Panameña* to graduate with a law degree, and when restrictions were lifted, she became the first female lawyer to practice law.

Clara also co-founded the *Partido Nacional Feminista* (PNF) as another way of "promoting women's rights and suffrage." She also travelled to the United States and earned a doctorate from New York University, and joined the Inter-American Commission of Women, led by Doris Stevens, as the representative for Panamá.

There she headed the research of "the status of women's rights." She ultimately left because she thought that the organization was withholding funding and opportunities from its Latin American members.

When she returned to her home country, she began teaching economics, political science, and sociology at the University of Panamá. Through her fight for women's rights and child welfare, she became the first *Panameña* appointed as a juvenile court judge in the *Tribunal Tutelar de Menores*.

While she was able to do much for the children of Panamá, due to underfunding and understaffing, she wasn't able to achieve everything she hoped. She passed away in February 1990 due to complications from a hip surgery.

GWENDOLYN MARGARET LIZARRAGA, MBE: THE CHAMPION FOR WOMEN'S FINANCIAL FREEDOM

For many centuries, women often had to depend on the benevolence of the men in their lives for financial security. This was something that frequently found many women suffering destitution, poverty, or abuse. At least within the United States, it wasn't until 1862 that women were able to claim property in their own names. But, with all her wisdom and compassion, Gwendolyn, also known as Madam Liz, understood the freedom that came when women felt empowered financially.

At the time of her birth, on July 11, 1901, Belize was still referred to as British Honduras. Much of the work she did then laid the ground-work for the time when Belize gained independence from Great Britain in 1981. Madam Liz was a businesswoman who was passionate about women's rights, something that eventually led her into politics.

As an entrepreneur, she bucked tradition and built success her own way, not backing down from a bully and leading with compassion. Madam Liz was known for running a successful mahogany and chicle (a naturally occurring latex) farm. She was also said to be outspoken, drive a car, and wear pants (remember, this was the 1920s-30s).

In an interview, her grandson, Dr. Victor Lizarraga, spoke about her compassion and understanding of women's position within society. He noted how, when wives would come to complain about their husbands' paychecks not reaching the home, she began to pay the wives to ensure that the money was getting to where it needed to go. She also believed in equal pay for equal work regardless of the person's gender.

Gwendolyn's foray into government and politics first began in 1953, when she was hired as a parole officer by the Social Development Department. However, it wasn't until 1954 that she started organizing women across the country politically. This led to the creation of the United Women's Group in 1959, a group that supported women in their cultural, economic, and political aspects.

She also co-founded the United Women's Credit Union and encouraged women to save, since only landowners could vote in British Honduras. Madam Liz's love and passion for her fellow countrywomen made her a force to be reckoned with. When women were denied land, she was said to have marched into the swamps and marshes to plot out land.

When children in low-income areas were denied schools, she was said to have grabbed a group of women and started clearing out mangroves. In 1961, women were officially allowed to run in national elections, and Madam Liz became the first woman elected to the National Assembly. She held positions as Minister of Education, as well as Minister of Housing and Social Services. She was reelected for both positions in 1965 and 1969, respectively.

In 1974, she stepped down from her government position and subsequently passed in June 1975.

FELÍCITAS CHAVERRI MATAMOROS: THE STUDENT WHO ACHIEVED THE CAREER OF HER DREAMS

There was a time when women were only allowed to attend school to learn how to be better homemakers, so that they could improve the lives of those around them. But a life half-lived and half-learned was never on the books for Felícitas. For the Costa Rican-born Latina, pursuing her dream of higher education was something that she knew she would achieve.

Lita, as she was lovingly known, was born on May 9, 1894, in Atenas, before relocating with her family to Heredia. From an early age, she showed a strong passion for helping others and being of service to her community. This love and sense of vocation are what inspired her to pursue a university degree in pharmacy.

Not only was a woman wanting to go into pharmacy unheard of, a woman going into higher education was as well. Because it was something that had never been done before, Lita had to challenge her university's school of pharmacy governing board for her to enroll. While there were no regulations that expressly prohibited women from participating, Lita was trying to break with the upstanding norm that schooling was for men.

Because of her dream to become a pharmacist, her story spread and caught the attention of many. Eventually, the governing board ruled in her favor, she was able to enroll, and she graduated with a pharmacy degree in 1917. Upon receiving her degree, she became the first woman to graduate with an accredited professional degree in Costa Rica.

Lita went on to manage several pharmaceutical management companies as well as become the head of the Drugs and Narcotics Department within the Ministry of Public Health. In addition to her pioneering efforts for education and career-focused Costa Rican women, she was also a poet and published several works.

In the close to two decades that she spent as a pharmacist, Felícitas created lasting change for Costa Rican women who wanted to pursue pharmacy and continue their education. She passed away in October 1934, at just forty, in San José. In 2002, she was inducted into the Women's Gallery of the National Institute for Women in Costa Rica.

MATILDE HIDALGO NAVARRO DE PRÓCEL: *LA NIÑA QUE PUDO*

It isn't just anyone who can make history and change society's internalized limited beliefs about what is possible. Typically, it takes someone with vision and purpose who can see the long-lasting and widespread effects of their dreams. Mathilde was one of those kinds of women who understood that she didn't need to fall in line with what others did or said just because that was what was always done.

Born in Loja, Ecuador, on September 29, 1889, Matilde was one of six children born to a seamstress. Like many awesome Latinas, she was someone who showed a special aptitude for her studies from a young age. Upon finishing sixth grade, she dreamed of continuing to high school, something that came true despite being riddled with much strife, as some people in her community ostracized her.

Undeterred by the treatment she received from her peers, she excelled and on October 8, 1913, she became the first woman to graduate from high school in Ecuador. Now with the education bug deeply planted in her heart, she continued her education by going on to study medicine. That journey wasn't without its troubles, as the dean of the faculty of the school of medicine near her refused to admit her.

Not one to take no for an answer, she enrolled at the University of Azuay in 1919 and went on to graduate with a medical degree, earning honors. In 1921, she returned to Quito and enrolled in the Central University of Ecuador to complete her doctorate. Upon graduating, she became the first woman to earn a doctorate in Ecuador.

Like many spitfires, Matilde didn't just stop with her education and medical degrees; she also challenged the status quo further by announcing that she would be voting in the 1924 presidential elections. After much deliberation from within the government, she was allowed to vote. On June 9, 1924, she became the first woman to cast a vote in a national election in Latin America. This moment in history also marked Ecuador as the first country to allow women to vote on the continent.

Matilde also became the first female vice president in her local municipality's council and the first deputy elected to congress. She was awarded the National Merit Award in 1956 and 1971 by both the President and the Minister of Public Health of Ecuador.

The enterprising Latina was the founding member of both the Medical Federation of Ecuador and the Surgical Association of Quito. The Ecuadorian Red Cross granted her the esteemed title of Honorary Lifetime President in the El Oro province. After she died in 1974, her hometown of Loja established a museum in her honor, and she was awarded the Medal of Merit and the Medal of Public Health by governmental decree.

ADELAIDA CHAVERRI-POLINI: THE STAUNCH DEFENDER OF THE GREEN

Nature is humanity's most significant gift from the universe. A great deal can be derived from it, including sustenance, medicine, and environmental protection. As populations have grown, an increasing number of forests and natural habitats have been affected by deforestation and climate change. This is something that Adelaida spent an entire career working to reverse.

The tropical forest and conservationist was born in Costa Rica on May 21, 1947, and began her career after having studied both mathematics and biology at the University of Costa Rica. In the 1970s, she helped establish the Costa Rican Nature Conservation Association to help raise awareness of the importance of protecting local biodiversity and ecosystems. The primary focus of her work was on tropical forests and marshes.

Her tireless work also led her and her colleagues to convince the government to establish both the Chirripó National Park and the Corcovado National Park (which expanded the country's national park service). Over the years, Adelaida became a leading expert on the Chirripó National Park and even wrote the book "Historia Natural del Parque Nacional Chirripó."

Looking to ensure that she passed on her knowledge and love of conservation to the following generations, she became a lecturer at the School of Environmental Sciences at Universidad Nacional in Costa Rica. Adelaida was also a co-founder of the Monteverde Cloud Forest Preserve, which the Tropical Science Center runs, and it remains a highly studied phenomenon.

Along with her many scientific publications, her work led her to be regarded and recognized as one of the world's leading experts on the conservation of forests and marshes. Some of her work even contributed to the discovery of new fungus species. Adelaida passed away in September 2003, leaving behind a legacy of conservation and a body of work that forever changed how Costa Rica approached the protection of its forests.

In 2020, a special stamp was released to honor her contributions to her home country for International Women's Day.

"An authentic woman is not one who does not imitate anyone, but one whom no one can imitate."

MARÍA FÉLIX, A MEXICAN ACTRESS AND
POWERFUL FIGURE IN THE GOLDEN AGE OF
MEXICAN CINEMA WHO WAS RECOGNIZED AS
A STYLE ICON, A FEMINIST SYMBOL, AND
KNOWN FOR HER REFUSAL TO PLAY
STEREOTYPICAL ROLES OR LEARN ENGLISH
FOR HOLLYWOOD FILMS

NINE

CHAMPIONS OF THE LAND

ENVIRONMENTAL AND
COMMUNITY ACTIVISTS

As we have seen across the chapters of this book, Latinas have stood at the front lines of land, culture, and survival. They are and have always been community organizers, truth-tellers, and guardians of ancestral knowledge who defend their people and their environment against forces of violence, exploitation, and erasure. Some led marches in the face of armed insurgencies; others revived ancient practices, teaching younger generations to weave stories of resistance into every thread. Still others stood before governments and global institutions, demanding recognition of Indigenous rights and protection of sacred lands.

Their activism has taken many forms: organizing communal kitchens to feed the hungry, weaving *molas* and textiles that preserve cultural identity while sustaining local economies, testifying to atrocities that powerful governments tried to deny, and building all-women patrols to keep forests free from extractive industries. Creativity, organizing, and memory became weapons just as powerful as rifles or courts.

For their defiance, many faced threats, exile, or even death. Yet their courage transformed grief into movements, tradition into resilience, and communities into models of self-determination.

These women remind us that defending land and life is inseparable from defending dignity. They show that activism is not only protest:it is the daily act of cooking for neighbors, reviving languages, protecting rivers, or simply refusing to be silenced. They are proof that community power can resist even the most entrenched systems of violence and exploitation.

THE WOMEN OF GUNA YALA: GUIDING THE ISLANDS' FUTURE

Across the turquoise waters of Panama's Caribbean coast lies Guna Yala, a chain of more than three hundred islands where the Guna people have preserved their culture with remarkable resilience. In this archipelago, women are not only central to family and economic life; they are celebrated as the keepers of tradition, land, and identity. Their society, organized around a matrilineal system, ensures that property and inheritance pass through women, giving them a degree of economic power and social respect rare in the region. When a Guna man marries, he moves into his wife's household; from that point forward, his labor belongs to her family. It is women who decide how food and resources are distributed, placing them at the heart of community well-being.

This elevated status is visible in everyday life and ritual. The community's most important celebrations:birth, puberty, and marriage:are all centered on women. The puberty ceremony, *inna suit*, marks a girl's transition into adulthood with song, dance, and the piercing of her septum for a golden ring:symbol of her value and strength. Such traditions reaffirm, from an early age, the respect accorded to women in Guna society.

Economically, women drive the community forward. They are the primary creators of *molas*, intricate hand-stitched textiles that have become symbols of Guna identity and major sources of income. A single *mola* can earn more than a fisherman's day of labor, and through their art, women sustain both family finances and cultural continuity. Tourism has amplified this role: Guna women are now entrepreneurs, selling crafts, running small businesses, and forming cooperatives to protect their heritage from outside exploitation.

Equally striking is Guna Yala's openness to gender diversity. Within their worldview, the *Omeggid*:literally "like a woman":form a respected "third gender." Boys who display feminine tendencies are free to grow up as women, often mastering *molas* and other female-associated roles. This tradition, rooted in Guna mythology, illustrates a society where identity comes from the heart, not imposed rules. While Western influence has begun to introduce prejudice, the islands still embody a rare cultural embrace of gender fluidity, echoing Indigenous traditions worldwide.

What is perhaps most impressive is how such a small and remote community has held onto these progressive values despite centuries of outside pressure. The Guna show that equity and respect are not lofty ideals, but daily practices woven into family, ritual, and economy. Their example proves that by honoring women, protecting identity, and embracing difference, even the tiniest island society can model a more just and sustainable way of life:one the wider world would do well to learn from.

RUFINA AMAYA: THE VOICE OF EL MOZOTE

Rufina Amaya Márquez (1942–2007) carried the memory of one of the darkest chapters in Latin American history. Known as the last survivor of the El Mozote massacre, she became the living testimony of a crime that El Salvador's government, and even the United States, attempted to deny for more than a decade. Her courage in reliving her trauma and telling the truth made her not only a symbol of resistance, but also a voice for hundreds of silenced victims.

On December 11, 1981, US-trained soldiers from the Atlacatl Battalion entered the village of El Mozote, a small rural community in Morazán province. In the midst of El Salvador's brutal civil war, the army suspected that peasants were aiding leftist guerrillas. Without evidence, they launched a massacre that became the single largest killing of civilians in the Western Hemisphere in modern times. Over the course of hours, more than eight hundred men, women, and children were executed:many brutally tortured, raped, or burned alive.

Amaya, then a thirty-nine-year-old mother of five, was among the last group of women rounded up. As soldiers prepared to kill them, she managed to slip behind a tree and hide. From there, she witnessed unspeakable horrors: men being beheaded, women assaulted, and children slaughtered. Most devastating of all, she heard the voices of her own children crying out for her moments before they were killed. Her husband, who was blind, was also murdered.

For months, Amaya lived in hiding, eventually finding refuge in a Honduran camp. There, she became a lay pastor and slowly began telling her story. In early 1982, she gave her first testimonies to journalists from *The New York Times* and *The Washington Post*. At the time, the Reagan administration, which supported the Salvadoran military, dismissed the reports. Amaya was called a liar by officials and conservative media outlets. Yet she persisted, repeating her testimony to human rights investigators and church groups.

A decade later, a United Nations truth commission ordered forensic exhumations in El Mozote. The Argentine Forensic Anthropology Team confirmed what Amaya had always said: hundreds of bodies, including those of children, lay in mass graves. The massacre was no longer in dispute, and her testimony stood as the most powerful first-hand account of the atrocity.

Rufina Amaya died of a stroke in 2007 at the age of sixty-four. She left behind not only the memory of her family, but also a moral legacy: that the world must never forget El Mozote. Today, her voice continues to echo as both a reminder of the cruelty of war and a testament to the strength of survival and truth.

NILDA CALLAÑAUPA ALVAREZ: WEAVING CULTURE AND COMMUNITY

Nilda Callañaupa Alvarez, a Quechua weaver, scholar, and community leader, has dedicated her life to safeguarding and revitalizing the textile traditions of the Peruvian Andes. Born in the small highland village of Chinchero, Nilda grew up tending her family's sheep and learning to spin and weave while watching over them in the fields. What began as a childhood pastime became a lifelong calling: to rescue the intricate techniques of her ancestors from the brink of disappearance and ensure they remain a living practice for generations to come.

From an early age, Nilda was fascinated by the textiles of her elders. While many women of her mother's generation wove for tourists with synthetic yarns and dyes, she sought out the grandmothers who still worked in the traditional ways, begging them to share their knowledge. Her father, a traveling trader, often brought back old cloth from distant regions, further fueling her curiosity. By her teenage years, with encouragement from anthropologists and ethnobotanists who recognized her talent, Nilda committed herself to reviving her community's weaving heritage.

Breaking barriers, she became the first person from Chinchero to attend college, and later traveled to the United States, where she studied English and began building connections with an international community of weavers and scholars. These experiences broadened her vision and gave her the tools to amplify the voices of Andean artisans on the world stage.

In the 1990s, Nilda co-founded the *Centro de Textiles Tradicionales del Cusco* (CTTC), which now supports ten Andean villages, each with its own weaving traditions. Under her leadership, the CTTC has spearheaded the recovery of endangered techniques such as *watay* (ikat warp patterns), *ticlla* (tie-dyed cloth), doubleweave, and cross-knit looping, many of which had nearly vanished. By reintroducing the use of natural dyes like cochineal and indigo, the Center has also reinforced both ecological sustainability and cultural pride.

Central to Nilda's mission is education. Through the Young Weavers groups in each community, children and teenagers learn spinning, dyeing, and weaving alongside elders, creating an intergenerational chain of knowledge. For Nilda, these efforts are not just about craft, but about identity: Andean textiles embody sacred landscapes, honor Pachamama (Mother Earth), and preserve stories of animals, plants, and people woven into every design.

Now internationally recognized as an author, speaker, and expert on Cusqueñan textiles, Nilda remains rooted in Chinchero. Her dream, as she often says, is simple yet profound: to return home, sit with her family, and weave. Through her vision and determination, she has ensured that weaving endures not as a relic of the past, but as a vital and evolving expression of Andean culture.

MARÍA ELENA MOYANO DELGADO: *MADRE CORAJE* OF VILLA EL SALVADOR

María Elena Moyano Delgado (1958–1992), remembered as *Madre Coraje* ("Mother Courage"), was one of the most important grassroots leaders in modern Peruvian history. Her life's work defending women, children, and marginalized communities stood in stark contrast to the terror that engulfed Peru during the 1980s and early 1990s. Her brutal assassination at the hands of the Shining Path (*Sendero Luminoso*) made her a national symbol of resistance, dignity, and collective strength.

Born in Barranco, Lima, Moyano moved with her family in the early 1970s to Villa El Salvador, one of Lima's *pueblos jóvenes*:self-organized migrant settlements that would later become internationally recognized for their model of participatory democracy. Immersed in community struggles from a young age, Moyano studied sociology at Garcilaso de la Vega University while volunteering as a teacher and participating in social movements. Her political views evolved toward socialism, but her commitment was always pragmatic: fighting for the daily survival and empowerment of her neighbors, especially women.

By the 1980s, Moyano had emerged as a key organizer of mothers' clubs and the *Vaso de Leche* program, which sought to combat child malnutrition by guaranteeing a daily glass of milk. She rose to become president of the Women's Federation of Villa El Salvador (FEPOMUVES), which coordinated thousands of women in communal kitchens, health initiatives, and neighborhood projects. In 1989, she was also elected deputy mayor of Villa El Salvador with the United Left Party, balancing grassroots leadership with political office.

Her growing visibility made her a target for the Shining Path, which viewed social programs as threats to its revolutionary project. The group accused her of corruption and collaboration with the state, distributing pamphlets denouncing her. Moyano did not retreat. Instead, she publicly denounced both state repression and the insurgency's violence, insisting that the true revolution must affirm life, dignity, and community:not death and fanaticism.

On February 14, 1992, Moyano defied a Shining Path–declared "armed strike" by leading a *Marcha por la Paz* (March for Peace). The next day, she was assassinated during a community fundraiser; her body was desecrated with explosives as her children looked on. She was just thirty-three.

More than three hundred thousand people attended her funeral, and her murder marked a turning point in public opinion, stripping the Shining Path of what little support it had left. Moyano's legacy lives on in memoirs, films, murals, and community institutions that honor her courage.

Her words endure as a reminder: "The revolution is an affirmation of life and of collective dignity."

"When people hear me sing, I want them to be happy, happy, happy. I don't want them thinking about when there's not any money, or when there's fighting at home. My message is always felicidad:happiness."

CELIA CRUZ, AFRO-CUBAN SINGER AND
GLOBAL LATIN MUSIC ICON KNOWN AS THE
"QUEEN OF SALSA" FOR HER POWERFUL
VOCALS AND ENERGETIC PERFORMANCES

TEN
MATRIARCHS OF MOVEMENTS
LEADERS SHAPING SOCIETY

Movements are born from a place of heart, grit, and tenacity. There is also a deep understanding that there is strength in numbers. When we unite with our *hermanas*, there is a power and comprehension in that kinship that can, will, and has moved mountains. Pakistani activist and Nobel Peace Prize laureate Malala Yousafzai once said, "I think realizing that you're not alone, that you are standing with millions of your sisters around the world, is vital."

To be seen by your sisters, to walk hand in hand with them as you tear down the walls that for so long sought to keep you out:nothing can replace that force. Understanding that what you do can have ramifications beyond what you might expect or plan for is a quality that many lack. The mothers of movements don't fight the unseen forces for their own glory, but the glory of an entire people.

The women in this chapter birthed movements that went on to benefit not just the sisters they would never meet, but the societies that thought they could make the mistake of devaluing their worth.

PILAR JORGE DE TELLA: THE ADVOCATE FOR WOMEN & CHILDREN'S RIGHTS

Can it really be called a democracy if not everyone is allowed to vote? This might have been a question that Pilar Jorge de Tella asked her fellow Cubans as she led the suffrage movement in her country. Born in 1884 in Pinar del Río during the Spanish occupancy of Cuba, Pilar fought hard to ensure that every woman had the right to vote (whether they wanted to or not).

Active during the 1920s, the Cuban suffragist co-founded the influential Feminine Club of Cuba and the National Women's Congress, which debated important issues, strategies, and policies they sought to implement within the country. During one of her many passionate speeches to the Cuban Congress, Pilar uttered words that would immortalize her: "No one can deny that suffrage is the guarantee that reaffirms the identity of the individual."

Many of her stances and beliefs for her fellow *hermanas* were noted as controversial as she was fighting for things like "universal suffrage, access to birth control, education, child care, and better labor conditions as well as protections for children born out of wedlock."

Like many suffragists and activists of the time, Pilar spent some time at a women's correctional facility. One time in particular, she, along with Ana Quintana, Leonora Ferreira, and another suffragette, was arrested in the alleged bombing of a Cuban representative's home.

Given the decade she was heavily active in, many of those ideas seemed radical, but the determination to achieve what had never been done before eventually bore fruit. In 1934, the women of Cuba, which was no longer under Spanish occupation, were given the right to vote. Once this was achieved, it was said that she stepped away from the political arena. She passed away in April 1967, leaving behind a powerful legacy.

MATILDE OBARRIO DE MALLET: THE CHAMPION FOR PUBLIC HEALTH IN TIMES OF CRISIS

An extension of universal human rights is the ability to live in a healthy and safe society. When faced with the realities of war's remnants, post-Panama Canal construction, Ecuadorian-born Matilde knew she had to do something to help those left suffering. Born in March 1872, Matilde, who was married to Sir Claude Coventry Mallet, the British ambassador to Panama and Costa Rica, witnessed firsthand the destitute conditions and the widespread diseases in the Canal area.

Matilde had seen the sweeping change and help that the Red Cross in Europe was able to provide for people during and after World War I. She felt that establishing a local branch would greatly benefit the people of Panama. Driven by a desire to create change and improve conditions in the area, she gathered several influential people and requested an audience with President Ramón Maximiliano Valdés.

Upon his approval and the passage of Law No. 40, Matilde was able to move forward with her plans, and thus established the National Red Cross of the Republic of Panama in 1917. The organization's goal was to care for the sick and injured affected by natural disasters or epidemics.

Among her many accomplishments, the Panamanian branch of the Red Cross was equipped to conduct tens of thousands of home visits on hygienic practices, treat over six hundred children, perform over fourteen thousand health examinations, and establish a tuberculosis clinic that treated patients effectively. She was able to achieve all of this within one year.

Unfortunately, at the one-year mark, she had to step down from her role as the founder and manager of Panama's Red Cross branch, as her husband was relocated to another country for work. She passed away in 1964 in the United Kingdom.

VIOLETA BARRIOS DE CHAMORRO: *LA DOÑA DE NICARAGUA*

Being the first to do something is never easy. It often requires an untold amount of grit, strength, courage, and bravery. Latinas who break through the glass ceiling are usually the ones who carry the silent shards of injustice.

When Violeta embarked on her journey as a journalist, it is likely that she never foresaw the way her life would unfold. But she eventually became a beacon for speaking out against oppression regardless of what would happen, simply because it was the right thing to do.

The Nicaraguan-born journalist-turned-politician was born to a wealthy family in Rivas on October 18, 1929. Due to her privileged upbringing, she was able to spend the early years of her education at schools in both Texas and Virginia. In 1950, she returned to Nicaragua, and some time after, she married Pedro Joaquim Chamorro Cardenal.

Violeta went to work for her husband's newspaper, *La Prensa*, a publication that was critical of and often unsympathetic to the Somoza family dictatorship. Because of their outspoken articles, the Chamorros had to go into exile sometime in 1957, and for several years, they lived in Costa Rica until the Somoza government gave them amnesty. Unfortunately, Pedro was assassinated in 1978, something that sparked the Sandinista revolution:something that ultimately took down the Somoza government.

After becoming disillusioned by the Sandinista government and its policies, Violeta took over her late husband's newspaper and began speaking out about them. This put her and *La Prensa* on their watchlist and saw the publication shut down or banned from print. At the end of the Contra-Sandinista civil war, free elections were once again available to the people of Nicaragua.

In 1990, Violeta was nominated for the presidency and ultimately won, becoming the first female president in Nicaragua. During her presidency, Doña Violeta reversed a number of Sandinista policies, lifted censorship, and privatized several state-owned industries. Much of what she did during her term enabled the fragile peace and power balance after the civil war to steady itself.

In 1996, she published her autobiography, *DREAMS OF THE HEART: The Autobiography of President Violeta Barrios de Chamorro of Nicaragua*, which detailed her determination, desire, and drive to help her fellow countrypeople. When her term ended in 1997, she retired from politics and went on to live a private life.

She passed away on June 14, 2025, in Costa Rica, as she and her family once again had to go into exile from the Ortega regime. Because of her family's persecution, the Violeta Barrios de Chamorro Foundation had to close down in 2021 due to government censorship.

TERESA MARTÍNEZ DE VARELA: THE TENACIOUS POET WHO NEVER GAVE UP WRITING

Latinas across the board have experienced erasure to varying degrees:some Latinas more than others. Because of society's active participation in the treatment of women, authors like Teresa were often left out of the narrative due to the lack of understanding that people had about her work. But, like all the women within this book, that didn't stop her from creating her art.

Under the name Lisa de Andráfueda, Teresa went on to become the first Afro-Colombian woman to publish literary works in her home country. Born in Quibdó, the capital of Chocó, on July 1, 1913, she was born to an Afro-Colombian father and a mother of Spanish descent. From a young age, her mother encouraged her to read and to borrow books from her grandfather's library. This is said to have planted the seed of voracious reading and a love of literature in her heart.

Teresa was extremely passionate about writing, which led her to pen not just poetry but also essays about Colombian folklore and politics. She also authored novels, theatrical plays, anagrams, and biographies. She published six books, *Guerra y Amor*, *Mi Cristo Negro*, *El Papi Gamín*, *Cantos de Amor y Soledades: Obra Poética*, *Diego Luis Córdoba: Biografía*, and *Caravana de Periodistas por dentro y Odisea de los Cuna-Cunas de Darién*.

In addition to her literary works, she was an accomplished journalist, being the only woman to join the *Caravana Nacional de Periodistas del Chocó*, writing about racial issues that were prominent at the time. Teresa was a woman who rebelled against the societal constraints she faced and worked tirelessly to distance herself from the roles society wanted to place on her shoulders.

Because of her trailblazing mindset and manner of being, Teresa felt that she was largely misunderstood by the society she was surrounded by. While she received some recognition for her work, many of her writing projects have gone unpublished.

Teresa passed away in 1998 in Cali, and she was primarily known as the mother of Jairo Varela, founder of *Grupo Niche*. In 2009, Úrsula Mena Lozano published Teresa's biography, *En Honor a la Verdad*, spotlighting everything that the intrepid and fearless writer, poet, and journalist had contributed to Colombia's literary landscape.

MÓNICA RAMÍREZ: THE ACTIVIST AND LAWYER WHO SAID TIME'S UP

Whether we realize it or not, many movements are born in the hearts of Latinas long before they are even aware of it. When life intersects with injustice and violence, the need for equitable access to resources is more prominent and critical than ever. As a Latina who wears many hats, Mónica understands the true realities of the world and how that affects her community.

As an activist, civil rights attorney, entrepreneur, writer, and public speaker, she has worked tirelessly to bring adequate resources to migrant communities and fight to eliminate gender-based violence. As the daughter and granddaughter of migrant farmworkers, born in a rural community in Ohio in the late 1970s, she has leveraged her platform to amplify the voices of those who would otherwise remain unheard.

Her work started in the early 2000s with a legal project that addressed gender discrimination towards female farmworkers, which evolved into Esperanza: The Immigrant Women's Legal Initiative of the Southern Poverty Law Center.

The insightful and visionary Latina has founded organizations such as Justice for Migrant Women, *Poderistas*, the Raizado Festival, The Latinx House, and co-founded the *Alianza Nacional de Campesinas*.

In 2017, she penned an open letter to the entertainment industry on behalf of Alianza, showing solidarity with the women and men who spoke out about and against gender-based violence within Hollywood. Her letter is credited as a catalyst for the TIME'S UP movement that sought to shine a light on the sexual assault experiences of women everywhere.

The Ohio-born Latina has received awards such as the Feminist Majority's Global Women's Rights Award, the Smithsonian's 2018 Ingenuity Award for Social Progress, and Harvard's Kennedy School's inaugural Gender Equity Changemaker Award.

Mónica has also lent her voice to the #QueridaFamilia letter (alongside America Ferrera, Diane Guerrero, and Eva Longoria) to further show her commitment and support for her community in a divisive political climate negatively affecting the Latino and Latine communities.

"It's because I'm so stubborn that I still insist on changing the world."

MERCEDES SOSA, AN ARGENTINE SINGER OF INDIGENOUS DESCENT WHO HELPED USHER IN THE "NUEVA CANCIÓN" MOVEMENT THAT REVITALIZED LATIN AMERICAN MUSIC AND HERALDED THE EMERGENCE OF MUSIC WITH INTENSE SOCIAL AND HUMANITARIAN MESSAGES ACROSS LATIN AMERICA

AFTERWORD

While this book is filled with tremendous, magnificent, and truly awesome Latinas, there are so many more out there that we weren't able to include. So many more who deserve to have a light shined on their greatness, their power, and their truth. So many more who have been quietly tucked away in the passage of time to such a degree that their existence is a mystery to the populace.

The power of Latinas lies in our ability to innovate when the chips are down and we feel like we have nothing else to lose and everything to gain. Latinas don't just fight for themselves, they fight for their collective sisterhood, their loved ones, and those yet to be born. They show up and show out regardless of what others will say.

Our hope is that, with this book, you feel inspired to hope, dream, and achieve. That you are reminded that, not only are you capable of what it takes to get where you want to go, but that you are deserving of it as well. Take this book as your starting point:a point of reference you can use on the days you find yourself full of doubt.

They say fortune favors the bold, and as sure as the sun will rise, the legacy that each of these women has created will stand the test of time, because in many cases, they have already. Remember, none of these women truly knew where their path would lead them, but just the same, they kept on.

And look at everything they accomplished.

The best part?

So can you.

.

REFERENCES

The sources and references used were active at the time of publication.

Introduction

Wilcox, Margaret A., et al. Inventions Created by Women. homepage.physics.uiowa.edu/~rmerlino/Inventions%20by%20Women.pdf.

Keepers of Justice: Activists and Advocates

Estela de Carlotto

Estela Barnes de Carlotto, "Interview with Estela Barnes de Carlotto, President of the Grandmothers of the Plaza de Mayo," interview by Vincent Bernard and Ximena Londoño, *International Review of the Red Cross* 99, no. 2 (2017): 487–95, https://doi.org/10.1017/S1816383118000358.

Abuelas de Plaza de Mayo, "Nuestra Historia," accessed September 1, 2025, https://www.abuelas.org.ar/historia.

Laura Inés Pollán Toledo

Bush Center. "Berta Soler: The Ladies in White." *Freedom Collection*. George W. Bush Presidential Center. Accessed March 15, 2025. https://www.bushcenter.org/freedom-collection/berta-soler-the-ladies-in-white.

Elisabeth Malkin, "Laura Pollán Toledo, Who Rallied Wives of Jailed Cuban Dissidents, Dies at 63," *New York Times*, October 15, 2011. Accessed March 15, 2025. https://www.nytimes.com/2011/10/16/world/americas/laura-pollan-toledo-who-rallied-wives-of-jailed-cuban-dissidents-dies-at-63.html.

"Laura Pollán, Leader of Cuba's White Ladies Group of Activists." *Independent*, October 21, 2011. Accessed March 15, 2025. https://www.independent.co.uk/news/obituaries/laura-pollan-leader-of-cuba-s-white-ladies-group-of-activists-2374308.html.

John Suarez San Martín, "The Case of Laura Pollán: Death by Purposeful Medical Neglect?" *Cuba Exile Quarter*, October 15, 2011. Accessed March 15, 2025. https://cubanexilequarter.blogspot.com/2011/10/case-of-laura-pollan-death-by.html.

Berta Cáceres

Nina Lakhani, "Who Killed Berta Cáceres? Behind the Brutal Murder of an Environment Crusader," *Guardian*, June 2, 2020. Accessed March 15, 2025. https://www.theguardian.com/world/2020/jun/02/who-killed-berta-caceres-behind-the-brutal-of-an-environment-crusader.

Zinn Education Project. "Berta Cáceres: Environmental Organizer." *Zinn Education Project*. Accessed March 15, 2025. https://www.zinnedproject.org/materials/berta-caceres-environmental-organizer/.

Global Witness. "Remembering Berta Cáceres: Seven Years On, the Fight for Justice Continues." *Global Witness*, March 2, 2023. Accessed March 15, 2025. https://globalwitness.org/en/campaigns/land-and-environmental-defenders/remembering-berta-caceres-seven-years-on-the-fight-for-justice-continues/.

UMKC Women's Center. "The Legacy of Berta Cáceres." *UMKC Women's Center Blog*, March 19, 2018. Accessed March 15, 2025. https://info.umkc.edu/womenc/2018/03/19/the-legacy-of-berta-caceres/.

Lucía Ixchíu

Nobel Women's Initiative. "Meet Lucía Ixchíu, Guatemala." *Nobel Women's Initiative*. Accessed March 15, 2025. https://www.nobelwomensinitiative.org/meet-lucia-ixchiu-guatemala.

Lucía Ixchíu, "Calling for Justice Through Art Has Put Me at Risk, But I Won't Be Silenced," *Global Citizen*, October 3, 2024. Accessed March 15, 2025. https://www.globalcitizen.org/en/content/calling-for-justice-through-art-has-put-me-at-risk/.

Bertha Oliva Nativí

"Bertha Oliva: '*Mi misión en esta tierra es defender los derechos humanos.*'" *UPV/EHU*, October 13, 2022. Accessed March 15, 2025. https://www.ehu.eus/es/web/campusa/-/bertha-oliva-mi-mision-en-esta-tierra-es-defender-los-derechos-humanos.

Oliva, Bertha. "Author Page." *The Real News Network*. Accessed March 15, 2025. https://therealnews.com/author/bertha-oliva.

"Interview with Bertha Oliva." *Friendship Office of the Americas*, January 2019. Accessed March 15, 2025. https://www.friendshipamericas.org/sites/default/files/2019.1Bertha%20Oliva.interview.pdf.

Eufrosina Cruz

Cruz Mendoza, Eufrosina. "How I Claimed the Rights Life Had Denied Me | Eufrosina Cruz Mendoza | TEDxCuauhtémoc." *Amara*, 2016. Accessed March 15, 2025. https://amara.org/videos/msfqHZnLAytk/en/1768777/.

"Eufrosina Cruz." *Those Who Inspire*. Accessed March 15, 2025. https://www.thosewhoinspire.com/meet-the-ip/eufrosina-cruz/.

"'To Be Seen, You Must Be Brave': Eufrosina Cruz on Changing the Narrative for

Indigenous Women in Mexico." *Wempower*. Accessed March 15, 2025. https://wempower.co/to-be-seen-you-must-be-brave/.

Arce, Catherine. "Three Indigenous Women Who Are Shaping the Region." *Council on Hemispheric Affairs*, February 28, 2018. Accessed March 15, 2025. https://coha.org/three-indigenous-women-who-are-shaping-the-region/.

Rigoberta Menchú

Teaching Central America. "We Indians Have No Childhood." *Teaching Central America*, Latino Studies, NYU. Accessed March 15, 2025. https://www.teaching-centralamerica.org/we-indians-have-no-childhood.

Archives of Women's Political Communication. "Rigoberta Menchú." Carrie Chapman Catt Center for Women and Politics, Iowa State University. Accessed March 15, 2025. https://awpc.cattcenter.iastate.edu/directory/rigoberta-menchu/.

The Nobel Prize. "Rigoberta Menchú Tum—Biographical." Nobel Prize Outreach, 1992. Accessed March 15, 2025. https://www.nobelprize.org/prizes/peace/1992/tum/biographical/.

Learning for Justice. "Rigoberta Menchú." *Learning for Justice*, Southern Poverty Law Center. Accessed March 15, 2025. https://www.learningforjustice.org/classroom-resources/texts/rigoberta-menchu.

Nobel Women's Initiative. "Rigoberta Menchú Tum." *Nobel Women's Initiative*. Accessed March 15, 2025. https://www.nobelwomensinitiative.org/rigobertamenchutum.

Karla Avelar

Feder, J. Lester, and Nicola Chávez Courtright. "Meet The Trans Sex Worker Who Transformed A Gang-Controlled Prison." BuzzFeed News, 8 Feb. 2015, https://www.buzzfeednews.com/article/lesterfeder/meet-the-trans-sex-worker-who-transformed-an-el-salvadoran-p.

"Human Rights Defenders Profile: Karla Avelar from El Salvador." International Service for Human Rights (ISHR), 19 Oct. 2017, https://ishr.ch/defender-stories/human-rights-defenders-profile-karla-avelar-from-el-salvador/.

"Karla Avelar." Martin Ennals Award for Human Rights Defenders, 2017, https://www.martinennalsaward.org/hrd/karla-avelar/.

Elizalde, Isabel Cristina. "The Mother of El Salvador's Trans-Rights Movement." Lenny Letter, 26 Jan. 2018, https://www.lennyletter.com/story/karla-avelar-el-salvador-trans-rights-movement#google_vignette.

Dolores Huerta

National Women's History Museum. "Dolores Huerta." Women's History, www.womenshistory.org/education-resources/biographies/dolores-huerta.

Dolores Huerta Foundation. "Dolores Huerta." Dolores Huerta Foundation, doloreshuerta.org/dolores-huerta/.

Godoy, Maria. "Dolores Huerta: The Civil Rights Icon Who Showed Farmworkers 'Sí Se Puede.'" NPR, 17 Sept. 2017, www.npr.org/sections/thesalt/2017/09/17/551490281/dolores-huerta-the-civil-rights-icon-who-showed-farmworkers-si-se-puede.

National Park Service. "Dolores Huerta." National Park Service, 6 Apr. 2022, www.nps.gov/people/dolores-huerta.htm.

Serafina Dávalos

Agencia Presentes. "Serafina Dávalos: *La Primera Abogada de Paraguay, Feminista y Lesbiana.*" Agencia Presentes, 9 Sept. 2022, https://agenciapresentes.org/2022/09/09/serafina-davalos-la-primera-abogada-de-paraguay-feminista-y-lesbiana/.

"Mujeres Bacanas: Serafina Dávalos (1877-1957)." *Mujeres Bacanas*, https://mujeresbacanas.com/serafina-davalos-1877-1957/.

Kuna Roga. "Serafina Dávalos." Kuna Roga, https://kunaroga.org/serafina-davalos/.

Literary Lights: Writers, Poets, and Storytellers

Gabriela Mistral

"Gabriela Mistral—Biographical—NobelPrize.org." NobelPrize.org, www.nobelprize.org/prizes/literature/1945/mistral/biographical.

"Gabriela Mistral." Poetry Foundation, www.poetryfoundation.org/poets/gabriela-mistral.

Canún, Nicole. "Books by Nobel Prize Winner Gabriela Mistral." Homeschool Spanish Academy, 4 Dec. 2021, www.spanish.academy/blog/books-by-nobel-prize-winner-gabriela-mistral.

"Biography: Gabriela Mistral." Biography: Gabriela Mistral, www.womenshistory.org/education-resources/biographies/gabriela-mistral.

The Editors of Encyclopaedia Britannica. "Gabriela Mistral | Biography, Poems and Nobel Prize." Encyclopedia Britannica, 14 Jan. 1999, www.britannica.com/biography/Gabriela-Mistral.

Isabel Allende

"Isabel Allende—Biography." Isabel Allende, www.isabelallende.com/en/home.

---. "Isabel Allende | Books, Awards, and the House of the Spirits." Encyclopedia Britannica, 5 Sept. 2025, www.britannica.com/biography/Isabel-Allende.

"Isabel Allende | CSU." The California State University, www.calstate.edu/impact-of-the-csu/alumni/Honorary-Degrees/Pages/isabel-allende.aspx.

"Isabel Allende | Penguin Random House." PenguinRandomhouse.com, 26 Aug. 2025, www.penguinrandomhouse.com/authors/417/isabel-allende.

Cristina Peri Rossi

Echevarría, Roberto González. "Cristina Peri Rossi | Biography, Books, and Facts." Encyclopedia Britannica, 19 July 2002, www.britannica.com/biography/Cristina-Peri-Rossi.

Cristina Peri Rossi: Biography. people.wku.edu/inma.pertusa/cristinaperirossi/bio.html.

AreaW3—www.areaw3.com. "Uruguayan Cristina Peri Rossi Receives the Highest Award in Spanish Literature—News." XXI, www.uruguayxxi.gub.uy/en/news/article/uruguayan-cristina-peri-rossi-receives-the-highest-award-in-spanish-literature.

Cristina Peri Rossi | SPAN 24524 Contemporary Women Writers in Latin America. voices.uchicago.edu/202402span24524/perfiles-biograficos/cristina-peri-rossi.

Julia de Burgos

"Julia De Burgos." Poetry Foundation, www.poetryfoundation.org/poets/julia-de-burgos.

Academy of American Poets. "Julia De Burgos." Poets.org, poets.org/poet/julia-de-burgos.

"Julia De Burgos | Research Starters | EBSCO Research." EBSCO, www.ebsco.com/research-starters/history/julia-de-burgos.

Guzmán, Will. "Julia De Burgos (1914-1953)." BlackPast.org, 22 May 2020, blackpast.org/african-american-history/julia-de-burgos-1914-1953.

Sor Juana Inés de la Cruz

Merrim, Stephanie. "Sor Juana Inés De La Cruz | Mexican Poet, Scholar and Feminist." Encyclopedia Britannica, 20 July 1998, www.britannica.com/biography/Sor-Juana-Ines-de-la-Cruz.

---. "Sor Juana Inés De La Cruz." Poets.org, poets.org/poet/sor-juana-ines-de-la-cruz.

Poetry Foundation. "Sor Juana Inés De La Cruz." Poetry Foundation, www.poetry foundation.org/poets/sor-juana.

Tharps, Lori. "Meet Sor Juana Inés De La Cruz: The Mexican Poet Who Gave up Her Freedom to Be a Writer—Reed, Write, and Create." Reed, Write, & Create, 28 Oct. 2024, reedwriteandcreate.com/blog/sor-juana-ines-cruz-mexican-writer-feminist.

—Lorgia García Peña
"Lorgia García Peña | Carnegie Corporation of New York." Carnegie Corporation of New York, www.carnegie.org/awards/honoree/lorgia-garcia-pena.

"Book Keynote Speaker Lorgia Garcia Pena | Outspoken Agency —Outspoken." Outspoken, www.outspokenagency.com/lorgia-garcia-pena.

Princeton University. "Lorgia García Peña." Department of African American Studies, aas.princeton.edu/people/lorgia-garcia-pena.

"Lorgia García Peña." Lorgia García Peña, www.lorgiagarciapena.com.

Mochkofsky, Graciela. "Why Lorgia García Peña Was Denied Tenure at Harvard." The New Yorker, 27 July 2021, www.newyorker.com/news/annals-of-education/why-lorgia-garcia-pena-was-denied-tenure-at-harvard.
Lola Rodríguez de Tió
---. "Lola Rodríguez De Tió" Poets.org, poets.org/poet/lola-rodriguez-de-tio.

"Lola Rodriguez De Tio—(AP World History: Modern)—Vocab, Definition, Explanations | Fiveable." Fiveable, fiveable.me/key-terms/ap-world/lola-rodriguez-de-tio.

Research Guides: World of 1898: International Perspectives on the Spanish American War: Lola Rodríguez De Tió. guides.loc.gov/world-of-1898/lola-rodriguez-tio.

"Lola Rodríguez De Tió." EcuRed, www.ecured.cu/Lola_Rodr%C3%ADguez_de_Ti%C3%B3.
Lola Rodríguez De Tió (1843–1924) | 1898: U.S. Imperial Visions and Revisions. 1898exhibition.si.edu/es/node/103.

"Lola Rodríguez De Tió | Research Starters | EBSCO Research." EBSCO, www.ebsco.com/research-starters/history/lola-rodriguez-de-tio.
Clorinda Matto de Turner
"Clorinda Matto De Turner | Research Starters | EBSCO Research." EBSCO, www.ebsco.com/research-starters/history/clorinda-matto-de-turner.

Matto De Turner, Clorinda (1852–1909) | Encyclopedia.com. www.encyclopedia. com/humanities/encyclopedias-almanacs-transcripts-and-maps/matto-de-turner-clorinda-1852-1909.

LibraryThing. "Clorinda Matto De Turner—Author Page." LibraryThing, www. librarything.com/author/turnerclorindamattod.

Voices for Change: Feminists and Political Trailblazers
Dr. Paulina Luisi
Ehrick, Christine. "From Feminism to Eugenics: The Case of the Uruguayan Doctor Paulina Luisi." Gender & History, vol. 22, no. 3, 2010, pp. 676–697.

Bustle Staff. "11 Overlooked Women from History, According to 10 Female Historians." Bustle, 6 Dec. 2018, https://www.bustle.com/life/11-overlooked-women-from-history-according-to-10-female-historians-15961727.
Sara Justo
Billiken Staff. "*Sara Justo fue una educadora argentina, la cuarta odontóloga del país y líder del movimiento feminista del siglo XX.*" Billiken, https://billiken.lat/ educadores/sara-justo-fue-una-educadora-argentina-la-cuarta-odontologa-del-pais-y-lider-del-movimiento-feminista-del-siglo-xx/.

Terzaghi, María Teresa. "*Las miradas de Alicia Moreau y Sara Justo sobre los derechos políticos femeninos en los albores del siglo XX.*" Universidad Nacional de La Plata, 2018, https://sedici.unlp.edu.ar/bitstream/handle/10915/94618/Documento_completo.pdf-PDFA.pdf?sequence=1&isAllowed=y.
Nuria Piera
Dominican Today Staff. "Nuria Piera Denounces Disinformation and Defamation in Digital Media." Dominican Today, 17 Feb. 2025, https://dominicantoday.com/dr/ local/2025/02/17/nuria-piera-denounces-disinformation-and-defamation-in-digi tal-media/.

Women in Journalism. "Dominican Republic: Investigative Journalist Nuria Piera Hacked with Pegasus Spyware." Women in Journalism, 12 May 2023, https:// www.womeninjournalism.org/threats-all/dominican-republic-investigative-jour nalist-nuria-piera-hacked-with-pegasus-spyware.

"Nuria Piera." EcuRed, https://www.ecured.cu/Nuria_Piera.
Ana Irma Rivera Lassén
Higher Heights for America PAC. "Ana Irma Rivera Lassén." Higher Heights for America PAC, https://www.higherheightsforamericapac.org/candidate/ana-irma-rivera-lassen/. Accessed 11 July 2025.

del Mar Quiles, Cristina. "Ana Irma Rivera Lassén: 'We Must Empower Ourselves as the Opposition We Represent.'" Centro de Periodismo Investigativo and Todas, 15

Nov. 2024, https://periodismoinvestigativo.com/2024/11/rivera-lassen-empower-ourselves/.

Argelia Laya

Chávez Alava, Andreína. "Argelia Laya: The Afro-Venezuelan Woman that Ignited Grassroots Feminist Struggles." Venezuelanalysis, 27 Nov. 2021, https://venezuel analysis.com/analysis/15394/.

Capire Staff. "Argelia Laya: A Black Communist Woman against the Tide." Capire, https://capiremov.org/en/experience/argelia-laya-a-black-communist-woman-against-the-tide/.

Clorinda Matto de Turner

"Clorinda Matto de Turner." EBSCO Research Starters, https://www.ebsco.com/research-starters/history/clorinda-matto-de-turner.

"Clorinda Matto de Turner Facts for Kids." Kiddle Encyclopedia, https://kids.kiddle.co/Clorinda_Matto_de_Turner.

Margarita Mbywangi

Eduardo Avila. "Paraguay: From Forced Labor to Indigenous Leader." Global Voices, July 19, 2012. https://globalvoices.org/2012/07/19/paraguay-from-forced-labor-to-indigenous-leader/

Webber, Jude. "My Name Is Margarita Mbywangi." Financial Times, June 28, 2009. https://www.ft.com/content/1f4e11f4-6475-11de-a13f-00144feabdc0

Glendinning, Lee, and agencies. "Paraguay: Former Slave Gets Cabinet Position." The Guardian, August 19, 2008. https://www.theguardian.com/world/2008/aug/19/paraguay

Prudencia Ayala

Yahoo Noticias. *"Prudencia Ayala, la primera mujer que aspiró a la Presidencia en América Latina."* Yahoo Noticias, March 8, 2023. https://es-us.noticias.yahoo.com/prudencia-ayala-primera-mujer-presidenta-america-latina-el-salvador-123120307.html

Penados, Álvaro. "Prudencia Ayala (1885–1936)." BlackPast, March 14, 2021. https://www.blackpast.org/global-african-history/prudencia-ayala-1885-1936/

López, Victor Hugo. "She Dared to Run: The Unlikely Story of Prudencia Ayala." Americas Quarterly, May 5, 2021. https://www.americasquarterly.org/article/she-dared-to-run-the-unlikely-story-of-prudencia-ayala/

Alexandria Ocasio-Cortez

"A Progressive Insurgent Just Pulled off the Biggest Democratic Primary Upset in Years." Mother Jones, www.motherjones.com/politics/2018/06/alexandria-ocasio-cortez-joe-crowley-primary-new-york.

The New York Times. "Alexandria Ocasio-Cortez: A 28-Year-Old Democratic Giant Slayer." The New York Times, 27 June 2017, www.nytimes.com/2018/06/27/nyregion/alexandria-ocasio-cortez.html.

QUARTZ, et al. "Alexandria Ocasio-Cortez Won a Prestigious Science-Fair Prize for Research Involving Free Radicals." QUARTZ, 20 July 2022, qz.com/1481551/alexandria-ocasio-cortez-won-a-2007-isef-science-fair-prize-for-her-microbiology-research.

Carrie Chapman Catt Center for Women and Politics. "Alexandria Ocasio-Cortez." Iowa State University: Archives of Women's Political Communication, awpc.catt center.iastate.edu/directory/alexandria-ocasio-cortez.

Segers, Grace. "How Alexandria Ocasio-Cortez Won the Race That Shocked the Country." City & State NY, 6 July 2021, www.cityandstateny.com/politics/2018/06/how-alexandria-ocasio-cortez-won-the-race-that-shocked-the-country/178323.

"New York House District 14 General Election Results 2024." NBC News, 22 Aug. 2025, www.nbcnews.com/politics/2024-elections/new-york-us-house-district-14-results.
Sonia Sotomayor
Oyez. "Sonia Sotomayor: Associate Justice of the Supreme Court of the United States." Oyez, www.oyez.org/justices/sonia_sotomayor.

Supreme Court Historical Society. "The Supreme Court: Justice Sonia Sotomayor | Supreme Court Historical Society." Supreme Court Historical Society, 28 Mar. 2022, supremecourthistory.org/supreme-court-justices/associate-justice-sonia-sotomayor.

Academy of Achievement. "Sonia Sotomayor | Academy of Achievement." Academy of Achievement, 2 May 2025, achievement.org/achiever/sonia-sotomayor.

"Justice Sonia Sotomayor." NYU School of Law, www.law.nyu.edu/centers/ija-oral-history/sotomayor.

Minds of Discovery: Pioneers of Science and Technology
Nicole Auil Gomez
World Wildlife Fund. "Meet 13 Women Making Waves in Conservation." World Wildlife Fund, 11 Feb. 2022, www.worldwildlife.org/stories/meet-13-women-making-waves-in-conservation.

"Panel in the Main Pavilion: Ridge to Reef Hosted by WWF and WCS—Sea of Life."

Sea of Life, 22 Nov. 2024, www.seaoflife.org/iwic2024/event-five-ntse7-np283-8bbfk-7lwsh.

Gomez, Nicole Auil. "In Belize, Women in Conservation Are Making a Difference | Blog | Nature | PBS." Nature, 18 Mar. 2021, www.pbs.org/wnet/nature/blog/womens-history-belize.

Whitley Fund for Nature. "Strengthening the Recovery of the Antillean Manatee, Belize | Whitley Award." Whitley Award, 24 Nov. 2021, whitleyaward.org/winners/antillean-manatee-belize.

ResearchGate. "Nicole Auil Gomez." ResearchGate, www.researchgate.net/profile/Nicole-Auil-Gomez.

"Nicole Auil Gomez, MSc.- Staff." Wildlife Conservation Society, belize.wcs.org/en-us/About-Us/Staff.aspx.
Sabrina Gonzalez Pasterski
Perimeter Institute. "Sabrina Pasterski—About." Perimeter Institute, perimeterinstitute.ca/people/sabrina-pasterski.

Wheeler, Koby. "Sabrina Gonzalez Pasterski: The Next Einstein in the Making—San Diego Squared." San Diego Squared, 21 Sept. 2023, sd2.org/sabrina-gonzalez-pasterski-the-next-einstein-in-the-making.

WebEasy Professional Avanquest Software. Sabrina Gonzalez Pasterski. physics-girl.com.

"Sabrina Gonzalez Pasterski." Helena, helena.org/members/sabrina-gonzalez-pasterski.

Sabrina Gonzalez Pasterski Facts for Kids. kids.kiddle.co/Sabrina_Gonzalez_Pasterski.
Katya Echazarreta
TIME. "Katya Echazarreta Fulfilled Her Dream of Going to Space. Now She's Paying It Forward." TIME, time.com/collections/latino-leaders-2025/7310761/katya-echazarreta.

"Kat Echazarreta." Kat Echazarreta | Website, www.katechazarreta.com/about.

"Katya Echazarreta—Space for Humanity." Space for Humanity, spaceforhumanity.org/about/team/katya-echazarreta.
Dr. Lya Imber de Coronil
Auditoria Interna peca. "Lya Ímber De Coronil." Scribd, www.scribd.com/document/852634488/Lya-Imber-de-Coronil.

Cantor, Astrid. "The Female Pioneers of Venezuelan Medicine | Caracas Chronicles." Caracas Chronicles, 28 Mar. 2020, www.caracaschronicles.com/2020/03/28/the-female-pioneers-of-venezuelan-medicine.

Sofía Imber. "Sofía Imber Entrevista a Lya Imber De Coronil." YouTube, 2 July 2018, www.youtube.com/watch?v=_wCQtbmdfzQ.

Lya Imber De Coronil | Fundación Bengoa. www.fundacionbengoa.org/novedades/publicaciones/biografias/lya-imber-de-coronil.
Ana Karen Ramirez
World Economic Forum. "Ana Karen Ramirez Tellez." World Economic Forum, www.weforum.org/people/ana-karen-ramirez-tellez.

Ana Karen Ramirez | Innovators Under 35. www.innovatorsunder35.com/the-list/ana-karen-ramirez.

EGADE Business School. "30 EXATEC EGADE: Ana Karen Ramírez (FTM-BA'18)." EGADE Business School, egade.tec.mx/en/blog/30-exatec-egade-ana-karen-ramirez-ftmba18.

Expansión. "Ana Karen Ramírez: La Mexicana Que Ganó Los Women in Tech Awards." Expansión, 22 Nov. 2023, expansion.mx/tecnologia/2023/11/22/ana-karen-ramirez-la-mexicana-que-gano-los-women-in-tech-awards.

Ramírez, Ana Karen. "Las Mujeres En La Ciencia." TED Talks, www.ted.com/talks/ana_karen_ramirez_las_mujeres_en_la_ciencia.
Adelaida Chaverri Polini
Kappelle, Maarten, and M. Cleef Antoine. Adelaida Chaverri-Polini. www.scielo.sa.cr/scielo.php?script=sci_arttext&pid=S0034-77442004000100001.

"Stamp: Adelaida Chaverri Polini, Biologist and Conservationist (Costa Rica 2020)." TouchStamps,   touchstamps.com/Stamp/Details/987449/adelaida-chaverri-polini-biologist-and-conservationist.

Books by Adelaida Chaverri Polini (Author of Historia Natural Del Parque Nacional Churripó   Costa   Rica).   www.goodreads.com/author/list/6879044. Adelaida_Chaverri_Polini.
Dr. Elma Kay
Sea of Life. "Panel in the Main Pavilion: Ridge to Reef Hosted by WWF and WCS—Sea of Life." Sea of Life, 22 Nov. 2024, www.seaoflife.org/iwic2024/event-five-ntse7-np283-8bbfk-7lwsh.

Sanchez, Natalia. "Meet the Female Guardians Leading Belize's Conservation." Journeys With Purpose, 11 Dec. 2024, journeyswithpurpose.org/a-greener-future-the-female-guardians-saving-belize.

Allies, Wild Earth. "Voices From the Field: Elma Kay, Ph.D., of the University of Belize Environmental Research Institute—Wild Earth Allies." Wild Earth Allies, 18 Aug. 2023, wildearthallies.org/voices-elma-kay.

"Elma Kay." Re:Wild, www.rewild.org/team/elma-kay.

Dr. Ellen Ochoa
"Ellen Ochoa—NASA: Johnson Space Center Director, 2013—2018." NASA, www.nasa.gov/people/ellen-ochoa.

Women & The American Story. "Life Story: Ellen Ochoa (1958–): The Story of a Scientist Who Became the First Latina in Space." Women & the American Story, wams.nyhistory.org/end-of-the-twentieth-century/the-information-age/ellen-ochoa.

Britannica. "Ellen Ochoa: American Astronaut and Administrator." Britannica, www.britannica.com/biography/Ellen-Ochoa.

"Ellen Ochoa—Kennedy Space Center Visitor Complex." Kennedy Space Center Visitor Complex, www.kennedyspacecenter.com/person/ellen-ochoa.

"Barbie Inspiring Women Ellen Ochoa Doll." Mattel Creations, creations.mattel.com/products/ellen-ochoa-barbie-inspiring-women-doll-jbj28?srsltid=AfmBOorSYd4NEPEPtEsy9GBi71fBRQ7ZIPtUXh2lFnhMC8T8_ZxlDIFY.

Guardians of Culture: Musicians, Artists, and Creatives
Chiquinha Gonzaga
Donne—Women in Music. "Gonzaga, Chiquinha." Donne UK, https://donne-uk.org/author/gonzaga-chiquinha/.

Classic FM Staff. "Chiquinha Gonzaga: Brazil's First Woman Conductor Who Fought for Freedom with Music." Classic FM, https://www.classicfm.com/discover-music/chiquinha-gonzaga-brazil-first-woman-conductor-choro-composer/.

Instituto Moreira Salles. "Chiquinha Gonzaga, a Brazilian Woman Composer Is Born." Google Arts & Culture, https://artsandculture.google.com/story/chiquinha-gonzaga-a-brazilian-woman-composer-is-born-instituto-moreira-salles/5wWxoZrCxThmLw?hl=en.
Teresa Carreño

Steinway & Sons, "Teresa Carreño," Steinway & Sons Artists, accessed September 1, 2025, https://www.steinway.com/artists/teresa-carreno

West Chester University of Pennsylvania, "Teresa Carreño," Music in the Margins (blog), accessed September 1, 2025, https://library.wcupa.edu/musicinthemar gins/blog/TERESA-CARRENO

Encyclopaedia Britannica, "Piano," Encyclopaedia Britannica, last modified December 5, 2024, https://www.britannica.com/art/piano
Omara Portuondo
Blue Note Jazz Club. "Omara Portuondo." Blue Note New York, https://www. bluenotejazz.com/nyc/shows/?eid=TWL6809301.

Los Angeles Philharmonic Association. "Omara Portuondo." LA Phil, https://www. laphil.com/musicdb/artists/4287/omara-portuondo.
Sara Gómez
Richard Brody, "The Brief and Brilliant Career of Sara Gómez," The New Yorker, August 10, 2023, https://www.newyorker.com/culture/the-front-row/the-brief-and-brilliant-career-of-sara-gomez

Rebeca Schiller, "Sara Gómez: The Filmmaker Who Made the Invisible Visible in Post-Revolution Cuba," Golden Globes, March 28, 2022, https://goldenglobes.com/arti cles/sara-gomez-filmmaker-who-made-invisible-visible-post-revolution-cuba/
June Beer
Quixote Center. "BHM Series: Afro-Nicaraguan Artist & Poet June Beer." Quixote Center, February 9, 2021. https://quixote.org/bhm-series-afro-nicaraguan-artist-poet-june-beer

AWARE: Archives of Women Artists, Research and Exhibitions. "June Beer." AWARE Women Artists, accessed August 30, 2025. https://awarewomenartists. com/en/artiste/june-beer/

Tal Día Como Hoy. "June Beer (1935–1986)." Tal Día Como Hoy, May 17, 2023. https://www.taldiacomohoy.es/post/june-beer-1935-1986
Paz Errázuriz
Hammer Museum. "Paz Errázuriz." Radical Women: Latin American Art, 1960–1985, accessed August 30, 2025. https://hammer.ucla.edu/radical-women/artists/paz-errazuriz

Fundación MAPFRE. "Paz Errázuriz." Fundación MAPFRE, accessed August 30, 2025.   https://www.fundacionmapfre.org/en/art-and-culture/collections/paz-errazuriz/

Tom Seymour. "Photographer Paz Errázuriz Opens Long Overdue Retrospective." The Art Newspaper, July 29, 2025. https://www.theartnewspaper.com/2025/07/29/photographer-paz-errazuriz-opens-long-overdue-retrospective

Rita Moreno

National Women's History Museum. "Rita Moreno." Women's History, accessed August 31, 2025. https://www.womenshistory.org/education-resources/biographies/rita-moreno

Rita Moreno. "Rita Moreno." TIME: Firsts, accessed August 31, 2025. https://time.com/collection/firsts/4898542/rita-moreno-firsts/

On The Stage. "The Remarkable Journey of EGOT Winner Rita Moreno." On The Stage, accessed August 31, 2025. https://onthestage.com/blog/the-remarkable-journey-of-egot-winner-rita-moreno/

PBS. "Stream Rita Moreno: Just a Girl Who Decided to Go for It." American Masters, accessed August 31, 2025. https://www.pbs.org/wnet/americanmasters/stream-rita-moreno-documentary/11654/

Gans, Andrew. "Rita Moreno Named Recipient of Peabody Career Achievement Award." Playbill, 5 Jan. 2022, playbill.com/article/rita-moreno-named-recipient-of-peabody-career-achievement-award.

Renata Flores

Peru Travel. "Renata Flores: The Strength of Andean Musical Fusion." Peru.info, accessed August 31, 2025. https://peru.info/en-us/talent/blogperu/6/25/renata-flores-the-strength-of-andean-musical-fusion

Stephany Torres for Refinery29 Somos. "How Renata Flores Is Using Quechua To Make The Music Industry More Inclusive." Refinery29, October 6, 2020. https://www.refinery29.com/en-us/2020/10/10036118/renata-flores-peru-quechuan-music-indigineous-culture

Rosa Chávez Yacila. "Renata Flores Brought Quechua to YouTube, and Then Everything Changed." VICE, October 30, 2019. https://www.vice.com/en/article/renata-flores-brought-quechua-to-youtube-and-then-everything-changed/

Frida Kahlo

FridaKahlo.org. "Frida Kahlo and Her Paintings." FridaKahlo.org, www.fridakahlo.org.

Museum of Modern Art. "Frida Kahlo: Mexican, 1907–1954." MoMA, www.moma.org/artists/2963-frida-kahlo.

"Frida Kahlo | Artist Profile | National Museum of Women in the Arts." National Museum of Women in the Arts, 30 June 2022, nmwa.org/art/artists/frida-kahlo.

Britannica, and Alicja Zelazko. "Frida Kahlo: Mexican Painter." Britannica, www.britannica.com/biography/Frida-Kahlo.

CNN, and Lianne Kolirin. "Frida Kahlo Self-portrait Sells for $54.7 Million, Setting New Record for Female Artists." CNN, www.cnn.com/2025/11/20/style/frida-kahlo-portrait-record-woman-scli-intl.

America Ferrera

Harness. "America Ferrera—Harness." Harness, 20 Feb. 2024, iwillharness.com/people/america-ferrera.

UN Migration. "America Ferrera: Actress, Director, Producer - IOM Global Goodwill Ambassador." IOM—UN Migration, www.iom.int/america-ferrera.

Britannica. "America Ferrera: American Actress, Producer, Director, and Activist." Britannica, www.britannica.com/biography/America-Ferrera.

Ferrera, America. "My Identity Is a Superpower -- Not an Obstacle." TED Talks, 23 May 2019, www.ted.com/talks/america_ferrera_my_identity_is_a_superpower_not_an_obstacle.

kiddle. "America Ferrera Facts for Kids: Kids Encyclopedia Facts." Kiddle, kids.kiddle.co/America_Ferrera.

Mujeres Indomables: Athletes and Trailblazers in Sports

Marta Vieira da Silva

International Olympics Committee. "Marta Da Silva | Biography, Competitions, Wins and Medals." Olympics.com, www.olympics.com/en/athletes/marta.

"UN Women Goodwill Ambassador for Women and Girls in Sport Marta Vieira Da Silva." UN Women—Headquarters, www.unwomen.org/en/partnerships/goodwill-ambassadors/marta-vieira-da-silva.

Augustyn, and Adam. "Marta | Biography and Facts." Encyclopedia Britannica, 6 Aug. 2025, www.britannica.com/biography/Marta.

"In Brazil, Female Warriors Fight for a Level Playing Field." World Justice Project, worldjusticeproject.org/photo-essays/brazil-female-warriors-fight-level-playing-field.

Sylvia + Claudia Poll Ahrens

Wiki, Contributors to Olympics. "Silvia Poll." Olympics Wiki, olympics.fandom.com/wiki/Silvia_Poll.

Silvia Poll Biography | Pantheon. pantheon.world/profile/person/Silvia_Poll.

Times, Tico. "Costa Rican Poll Sisters Leave Lasting Olympic Legacy." The Tico Times | Costa Rica News | Travel | Real Estate, 26 July 2024, ticotimes.net/2024/07/26/costa-rican-poll-sisters-leave-lasting-olympic-legacy.

Ticos and Ticas: The People of Costa Rica. www.vacationscostarica.com/travel/ticos-costa-rica-people.

Olympedia—Sylvia Poll. www.olympedia.org/athletes/46201.

Olympedia—Claudia Poll. www.olympedia.org/athletes/46200.

Claudia Poll Biography | Pantheon. www.pantheon.world/profile/person/Claudia_Poll.

What Is the Origin of the Olympic Games? www.olympics.com/ioc/faq/history-and-origin-of-the-games/what-is-the-origin-of-the-olympic-games.
Marileidy Paulino
"Marileidy Paulino." Famous Birthdays, www.famousbirthdays.com/people/marileidy-paulino.html.

Usa, Hola! "Marileidy Paulino." HOLA! USA, 29 Sept. 2024, www.hola.com/us/latinapowerhouse/20240929712717/marileidy-paulino.

World Athletics. "Marileidy PAULINO—Athlete Overview." World Athletics, worldathletics.org/athletes/dominican-republic/marileidy-paulino-14749613.

Grand Slam Track. "Marileidy Paulino—Racer Profile." Grand Slam Track, www.grandslamtrack.com/competitors/marileidy-paulino.

Vazquez, Jennifer, NBC New York Staff. "Marileidy Paulino: What to Know About the First Dominican Woman to Win Gold—While Breaking an Olympic Record!" NBC New York, 9 Aug. 2024, www.nbcnewyork.com/paris-2024-summer-olympics/marileidy-paulino-dominican-republic-olympic-games-paris-facts/5688713.
Cholitas Luchadoras
Merritt, Asa. "Cholitas Luchadoras: The Indigenous Women Wrestlers of Bolivia | Only a Game." WBUR.org, 16 Jan. 2016, www.wbur.org/onlyagame/2016/01/16/cholitas-luchadoras-bolivia-women-wrestlers.

LaSota, Mark, PhD. "The Cholitas: Indigenous Women Athletes Paving the Way in

Bolivia." Forbes, 25 Dec. 2024, www.forbes.com/sites/marklasota/2024/12/25/the-cholitas-indigenous-women-athletes-paving-the-way-in-bolivia.

"Cholitas Bravas—Celia D. Luna | Miami Photographer | Professional Portrait | Self Portrait Photography." Celia D. Luna, www.celiadluna.com/cholitas-bravas.

Fontaine, Hannah. "Cholitas Luchadoras: Empowerment Inside and Outside the Ring." Latina Republic, 29 Sept. 2023, latinarepublic.com/2021/07/12/cholitas-luchadoras-empowerment-inside-and-outside-the-ring.

"Cholitas Wrestling/Cholitas Luchadoras." The Abroad Guide, theabroadguide.com/cholitas-wrestling-cholitas-luchadoras.

Tilden, Imogen. "Bolivia's Indigenous Female Wrestlers Mid-flight: Todd Antony's Best Photograph." The Guardian, 11 Aug. 2021, www.theguardian.com/artanddesign/2021/aug/11/bolivias-indigenous-female-wrestlers-mid-flight-todd-antonys-best-photograph.
Imilla Skate
Reporter, Guardian Staff. "ImillaSkate: An Indigenous Bolivian Skateboard Collective—Photo Essay." The Guardian, 22 Feb. 2022, www.theguardian.com/artanddesign/2022/feb/08/imillaskate-an-indigenous-bolivian-skateboard-collective-photo-essay.

"How Imilla Skate Celebrates Skateboarding's Indigenous Past and Present." Smithsonian Folklife Festival, festival.si.edu/blog/indigenous-skateboarding-culture.

"Whatever Happened to ... The Bolivian Women Who Skateboard in Indigenous Garb?" NPR, 2 Sept. 2024, www.npr.org/sections/goats-and-soda/2024/09/02/g-s1-20283/skateboard-bolivia-indigenous-women.
María Lorena Ramírez Hernández
Wef, By. "Lorena Ramírez: La Corredora Rarámuri Que Está Conquistando El Mundo Un Paso a La Vez." WEF Iberoamérica, 19 Feb. 2025, wefiberoamerica.org/actualidad/lorena-ramirez-la-corredora-raramuri-que-esta-conquistando-el-mundo-un-paso-a-la-vez.

María Lorena Ramírez Hernández. sites.ungeneva.org/not-a-womans-job/2023/en/permanent-missions/maria-lorena-ramirez-hernandez.html.

Marisa. "María Lorena Ramírez." Paraquetuveas, paraquetuveas.es/maria-lorena-ramirez.

Osegueda, Rodrigo. "Lorena Ramírez, Corredora Rarámuri, Representará a México En Ultramaratón De Hong Kong 100." México Desconocido, 14 Jan. 2025, www.mexicodesconocido.com.mx/lorena-ramirez-ultramaraton-de-hong-kong-100.html.

Rebels and Revolutionaries: Fighters for Freedom
Juana Azurduy de Padilla
Diplomat Magazine. "Juana Azurduy: Guerrilla of the Great Homeland." Diplomat
    Magazine, March 15, 2024. https://diplomatmagazine.eu/2024/03/15/juana-
    azurduy-guerrilla-of-the-great-homeland/

The Female Soldier. "Juana Azurduy." The Female Soldier, accessed August 31,
    2025. https://thefemalesoldier.com/blog/juana-azurduy

Montoya, Kaitlyn. "Juana Azurduy de Padilla and the Latin American Independence
    Movement." University of West Florida Research Repository, 2021. https://ircom
    mons.uwf.edu/esploro/outputs/eventposter/Juana-Azurduy-de-Padilla-and-the/
    99380090870606600

Policarpa Salavarrieta
Equality for Femmes Network. "Spotlight: Policarpa Salavarrieta and Colombian
    Women's Day." Equality for Femmes Network, November 14, 2023. https://www.
    eqfn.org/post/spotlight-policarpa-salavarrieta-and-colombian-women-s-day

Infinite Women. "Policarpa Salavarrieta." Infinite Women, accessed August 31, 2025.
    https://www.infinite-women.com/women/policarpa-salavarrieta/

BeLatina. "La Pola: The Colombian Revolutionary That History Books Almost
    Forgot." BeLatina, November 14, 2020. https://belatina.com/la-pola-colombian-
    revolutionary/
Hermelinda Urvina
Yalilé Loaiza, "Quién Fue Hermelinda Urvina, La Primera Mujer Sudamericana en
    Obtener una Licencia para Pilotar Aviones," Infobae, February 12, 2022, https://www.
    infobae.com/america/america-latina/2022/02/13/quien-fue-hermelinda-urvina-la-
    primera-mujer-sudamericana-en-obtener-una-licencia-para-pilotar-aviones/

Find A Grave, "Hermelinda Mayorga de Briones," accessed September 1, 2025,
    https://www.findagrave.com/memorial/30012071/hermelinda-mayorga_de_bri
    ones
Yuturi Warmi
Marie Eenens, "The Guardians of the Amazon: Yuturi Warmi's Fight Against Gold
    Mining," Green European Journal, August 26, 2025, https://www.greeneuropean
    journal.eu/the-guardians-of-the-amazon-yuturi-warmi/

Ana Maria Buitron, "The Indigenous Women Fighting Mining in Ecuador's Amazon,"
    BBC Future, May 3, 2024, https://www.bbc.com/future/article/20240503-the-
    indigenous-women-fighting-mining-in-ecuadors-amazon

Las Residentas

Kunaroga. "*Las Residentas de Ñeembucú.*" Kunaroga.org. Accessed September 1, 2025. https://kunaroga.org/las-residentas-de-neembucu/

Radialistas. "*Las Residentas.*" Radialistas Apasionadas y Apasionados. Accessed September 1, 2025. https://radialistas.net/las-residentas/

Salome Ureña de Henriquez

"Salomé Ureña de Henríquez." Poesía Dominicana. Accessed September 1, 2025. https://poesiadominicana.jmarcano.com/q-z/salome/

"Salomé Ureña de Henríquez." Antología de Poesía Dominicana. Accessed September 1, 2025. https://bookmaniac.org/poetry/antologia/salome-urena-de-henriquez/

"Biografía de Salomé Ureña." Biblioteca Virtual PUCMM. Pontificia Universidad Católica Madre y Maestra. Accessed September 1, 2025. https://opac.pucmm.edu.do/virtuales/salome/biografia.htm

Victoria Ocampo

Library of Congress. "Victoria Ocampo, Argentina, 1890–1979." Library of Congress Authorities & Vocabularies. Accessed September 1, 2025. https://www.loc.gov/item/n50035908/victoria-ocampo-argentina-1890-1979/

"Victoria Ocampo." Travel with Pen and Palate: Argentina. Accessed September 1, 2025. http://www.travel-with-pen-and-palate-argentina.com/victoriaocampo.html

Greenberg, Janet. "A Question of Blood: The Conflict of Sex and Class in the *Autobiografía* of Victoria Ocampo." In Victoria Ocampo: Writer, Feminist, Publisher, 130–147. Berkeley: University of California Press, 1995. https://publishing.cdlib.org/ucpressebooks/view?docId=ft7c600832&chunk.id=d0e4008&toc.depth=1&toc.id=d0e4008&brand=ucpress

Hidden Figures: Groundbreakers in Lesser-Known Fields

Clara González de Behringer

"Panama's Woman of the Century Lived in Santa Familia: The Story of Clara González de Behringer." Santa Familia, 21 September 2023, www.santafamiliapanama.com/news-updates/16/Panama%E2%80%99s+Woman+of+the+Century+Lived+in+Santa+Familia%3A+The+Story+of+Clara+Gonz%C3%A1lez+de+Behringer

"Clara González, 1898-1990." Wander Women Project, Accessed 9 March 2025, www.wanderwomenproject.com/women/clara-gonzalez/

Marco, Yolanda. "Clara González de Behringer: La protectora de la niñez." Pioneras de la Ciencia en Panamá, coordinated by Eugenia Rodríguez Blanco, Secretaría

Nacional de Ciencia, Tecnología e Innovación, SENACYT Centro Internacional de Estudios Políticos y Sociales, CIEPS AIP, 2022, pp. 30-40
Gwendolyn Margaret Lizarraga, MBE
Ros, Sokhunthea. "Six Dates in History That Changed Women's Financial Futures | Sound Credit Union." Sound Credit Union, 16 Sept. 2024, www.soundcu.com/blog/six-dates-in-history-that-changed-womens-financial-futures.

"Gwendolyn Lizarraga—Infinite Women." Infinite Women, 24 Jan. 2024, www.infinite-women.com/women/gwendolyn-lizarraga.

Gwendolyn Lizarraga, Date of Birth, Place of Birth, Date of Death. www.bornglorious.com/person/?pi=20983386.

Government of Belize Press Office. "Belizean Patriot: Gwendolyn Lizarraga." YouTube, 15 Sept. 2023, www.youtube.com/watch?v=Hpctsho-bnc.

Prezi, Angelica Figueroa On. "Gwendolyn Lizarraga: One of the Leaders in Belize's Nationalist Movement." prezi.com, prezi.com/p/qv-_l-jduovh/gwendolyn-lizarraga-one-of-the-leaders-in-belizes-nationalist-movement.
Felícitas Chaverri Matamoros
"Felícitas-Chaverri-Matamoros-galeria-de-las-mujeres—Instituto Nacional De Las Mujeres." Instituto Nacional De Las Mujeres, www.inamu.go.cr/es/-/contenido-fel%C3%ADcitas-chaverri-matamoros-galeria-de-las-mujeres.

Condega, Xavier. "Felícitas Chaverri Matamoros: La Primera Mujer Profesional En Costa Rica Fue Farmacéutica." El Mundo CR, 8 Aug. 2025, elmundo.cr/costa-rica/felicitas-chaverri-matamoros-la-primera-mujer-profesional-en-costa-rica-fue-farmaceutica.

Gutiérrez, Nuria and Escuela de Farmacia de Costa Rica. MATAMOROS: PRIMERA MUJER PROFESIONAL DE COSTA RICA. Illustrated by Grace Herrera, 2022, aurol.ucr.ac.cr/sites/default/files/2024-01/Edicion_54_noviembre_2022.pdf.
Matilde Hidalgo Navarro de Prócel
Richard. "Matilde Hidalgo De Prócel—Ecuadorian Literature." Ecuadorian Literature, 30 Apr. 2023, www.ecuadorianliterature.com/matilde-hidalgo-de-procel.

iFeminist. ifeminist.org/hidalgo.html.

Parfitt, Tom. "Matilde Hidalgo De Procel: Google Doodle Honours Ecuadorian Doctor and Activist." The Independent, 21 Nov. 2019, www.independent.co.uk/news/world/americas/matilde-hidalgo-de-procel-google-doodle-today-ecuador-doctor-death-who-a9211751.html.

Herbert, Tom. "Who Is Matilda Hidalgo De Procel? Today's Google Doodle Celebrates Trailblazing Activist | London Evening Standard." The Standard, 21 Nov. 2019, www.standard.co.uk/lifestyle/london-life/matilde-hidalgo-de-procel-google-doodle-activist-a4292541.html.

Adelaida Chaverri Polini

Kappelle, Maarten, and M. Cleef Antoine. Adelaida Chaverri-Polini. www.scielo.sa.cr/scielo.php?script=sci_arttext&pid=S0034-77442004000100001.

"Stamp: Adelaida Chaverri Polini, Biologist and Conservationist (Costa Rica 2020)." TouchStamps, touchstamps.com/Stamp/Details/987449/adelaida-chaverri-polini-biologist-and-conservationist.

Books by Adelaida Chaverri Polini (Author of Historia Natural Del Parque Nacional Churripó Costa Rica). www.goodreads.com/author/list/6879044.Adelaida_Chaverri_Polini.

Champions of the Land: Environmental and Community Activists

The Women of Guna Yala

Katka Lapelosová, "The Women of Guna Yala: The Islands Where Women Make the Rules," BBC Travel, August 13, 2018. https://www.bbc.com/travel/article/20180813-guna-yala-the-islands-where-women-make-the-rules

San Blas On Board. "The Role of Guna Women in the Local Economy and Culture." San Blas On Board. Accessed September 1, 2025. https://sanblasonboard.com/en/mujer-guna-yala/

Rufina Amaya

"Rufina Amaya, 64; Survivor of 1981 Massacre by Salvadoran Troops Spoke Out on the Slaughter," Los Angeles Times, March 13, 2007. https://www.latimes.com/archives/la-xpm-2007-mar-13-me-passings13.1-story.html

"Rufina Amaya: Survivor of El Mozote Massacre," NPR Morning Edition, March 13, 2007. Transcript. https://www.npr.org/transcripts/8972597

Alma Guillermoprieto, "Shedding Light on Humanity's Dark Side," The Washington Post, March 14, 2007. https://www.washingtonpost.com/archive/style/2007/03/14/shedding-light-on-humanitys-dark-side/9879ff73-8fbb-4287-8f75-7c7eed5c8796/

Nilda Callañaupa Alvarez

Aspen Institute. "Nilda Callañaupa Alvarez." Aspen Institute. Accessed September 1, 2025. https://www.aspeninstitute.org/people/nilda-callanaupa-alvarez/

Piecework Editorial Staff. "The Long Thread: Nilda Callañaupa Alvarez." Piecework Magazine, May 2, 2022. https://pieceworkmagazine.com/the-long-thread-nilda-callanaupa-alvarez/

The Metropolitan Museum of Art. "Weaving Together Generations." Perspectives. Accessed September 1, 2025. https://www.metmuseum.org/perspectives/weaving-together-generations

María Elena Moyano Delgado

Infobae. "María Elena Moyano, la mujer que le hizo frente a Sendero Luminoso." Infobae, September 9, 2022. https://www.infobae.com/america/peru/2022/09/09/maria-elena-moyano-la-mujer-que-le-hizo-frente-a-sendero-luminoso/

Pastor, Néstor David. "Remembering María Elena Moyano, 30 Years Later." NACLA, February 15, 2022. https://dev.nacla.org/remembering-maria-elena-moyano-30-years-later

Matriarchs of Movements: Leaders Shaping Society

Pilar Jorge de Tella

Cervantes, Cvc. Centro Virtual. CVC. La Mujer Revolucionaria Antes De La Revolución Cubana: Logros Y Vicisitudes, Por María Del Mar López Cabrales. cvc.cervantes.es/literatura/mujer_independencias/lopez.htm.

Noriega, Christina. "Herstory: 12 Cuban Women Who Changed the Course of History." Remezcla, 4 Apr. 2025, remezcla.com/lists/culture/cuban-herstory-womens-history-month.

"Pilar Jorge De Tella." DBpedia, dbpedia.org/page/Pilar_Jorge_de_Tella.

"Women Held in Cuban Fracas, the Iola Register (Iola, Kansas) 25 August 1931, P 1." Newspapers.com, 25 Aug. 1931, www.newspapers.com/article/the-iola-register-women-held-in-cuban-fr/47320 13.

Redacción Alma Mater. "Génesis Del Movimiento Feminista Cubano: Breve Acercamiento Al Primer Congreso Nacional De Mujeres." Medium, 7 Apr. 2023, medium.com/revista-alma-mater/g%C3%A9nesis-del-movimiento-feminista-cubano-breve-acercamiento-al-primer-congreso-nacional-de-mujeres-102c661584c9. Accessed 10 June 2025.

International Women's Day. "52 Inspirational Quotes for Women to Share Throughout the Year." International Women's Day, www.internationalwomensday.com/Missions/19614/52-inspirational-quotes-for-women-to-share-throughout-the-year.

Matilde Obarrio de Mallet

"Lady Matilde Mallet." GENi, 3 Jan. 2020, www.geni.com/people/Lady-Matilde-Mallet/6000000079429199316. Accessed 9 June 2025.

EcuRed. "Matilde Obarrio De Mallet." EcuRed, www.ecured.cu/Matilde_Obarrio_de_Mallet. Accessed 3 July 2025.

Panamatour.it. "Doña Matilde De Obarrio Vallarino De Mallet." Panamatour.it, panama-tour.site123.me/an%C3%A9cdotas-de-panam%C3%A1/do%C3%B1a-matilde-de-obarrio-vallarino-de-mallet. Accessed 3 July 2025.
Violeta Barrios de Chamorro
The Editors of Encyclopaedia Britannica. "Violeta Barrios De Chamorro | Biography and Facts." Encyclopedia Britannica, 6 Mar. 2003, www.britannica.com/biogra phy/Violeta-Barrios-de-Chamorro.

Politico. "Nicaragua's Former President Violeta Chamorro Dies at 95." Politico, 15 June 2025, www.politico.com/news/2025/06/15/nicaraguas-former-president-violeta-chamorro-dies-at-95-00406444.
Teresa Martínez de Varela
Oxford Reference. "Martínez De Varela, Teresa." Oxford Reference, www.oxfordrefer ence.com/display/10.1093/acref/9780199935796.001.0001/acref-9780199935796-e-1337.

EPFL. "Teresa Martínez De Varela." EPFL, graphsearch.epfl.ch/en/concept/ 56794287.

Mejia, Catalina. "Lisa De Andráfueda, Poet, Folklorist and Mother of Jairo Varela of the Niche Group—the Woman Post." The Woman Post, 15 Nov. 2022, thewoman post.com/2984/lisa-de-andrafueda-poet-folklorist-and-mother-of-jairo-varela-of-the-niche-group.

Teresa Martínez De Varela (Author of Mi Cristo Negro). www.goodreads.com/ author/show/22411037.Teresa_Mart_nez_de_Varela.
Monica Ramirez
Mónica Ramírez | Keynote Speaker | AAE Speakers Bureau. www.aaespeakers.com/ keynote-speakers/monica-ramirez.

National Women's Law Center. "Mónica Ramírez—National Women's Law Center." National Women's Law Center, 24 June 2025, nwlc.org/staff/monica-ramirez.

Ford Foundation. "Mónica Ramírez—Ford Foundation." Ford Foundation, 4 Apr. 2025, www.fordfoundation.org/fellows/monica-ramirez-2.

"Mónica Ramírez—Concordia." Concordia, 21 June 2022, www.concordia.net/ community/monica-ramirez.

Time. "700,000 Female Farmworkers Say They Stand With Hollywood Actors Against Sexual Assault." TIME, 10 Nov. 2017, time.com/5018813/farmworkers-solidarity-hollywood-sexual-assault.

ABOUT ASHLEY K. STOYANOV OJEDA

Ashley K. Stoyanov Ojeda is a first-generation Latina, business strategist, and the author of *Jefa in Training*. She runs a full-time consultancy focused on helping underrepresented entrepreneurs and thought leaders grow their businesses and amplify their voices. Through hands-on consulting, signature programs, and partnerships with government, nonprofit organizations and Fortune 500 companies, Ashley has supported thousands of changemakers on their leadership journey. When she's not building community, you can find her adventuring with her family in Portland, Oregon.

Website: www.ashleykstoyanovojeda.com

instagram.com/ashleykstoyanovojeda
threads.com/ashleykstoyanovojeda
tiktok.com/@ashleykstoyanovojeda
linkedin.com/ashleykervabon
thereframebyakso.substack.com

ABOUT MIRTLE PEÑA-CALDERÓN

Mirtle Peña-Calderón is a writer, editor, community builder, and Dominican firstborn daughter who is deeply committed to amplifying Latino and Latine voices and stories. As a journalist, she's been featured in *PEOPLE en Español, PEOPLE Magazine, HOLA! USA, FIERCE, mitú,* and other renowned platforms. As the founder of Latinidad Collective, a platform that celebrates culture, identity, and connection, she dives into themes of heritage, mental health, and the power of storytelling to heal and unite communities. When she's not writing, she loves to cook, be the fun *tía,* travel, and annoy her little brother (not all at the same time). *The Book of Awesome Latinas* is her debut book.

Website: www.mirtlepcalderon.com

instagram.com/mirtlepcalderon

threads.com/mirtlepcalderon

linkedin.com/in/mirtlenpenac

considerthisanote.substack.com

CONNECT WITH US!

We would like to thank you for joining us on this important journey through Latina history. This book was a huge labor of love and we hope that you've enjoyed reading and learning about all the amazingly awesome women we were able to mention in our book.

We are eternally grateful for your support and would love to hear what you thought of the book and how you felt after reading the stories of each of the women in it. Tell us what you loved, who you saw yourself reflected in, and what was your biggest takeaway.

Here are some ways to connect with us:

- Please post a review on Amazon. Each review that is shared helps us get closer to our dream of building more awareness of the amazing women we've featured.
- Active on Goodreads? We will be active on Goodreads after the book is published, so drop us a few lines.
- Got a thing for StoryGraph? Don't shy away from leaving us a review there either.
- Want to order books for your school or organization? Get in touch with our publisher, Books That Save Lives.
- Connect with us on our website + on our social channels to learn more about our work: